U0824980

汉英对照·汉语100点实用系列手册

生动汉语百例

100 Vivid Chinese Expressions

李　红　编著
孙　弢　译

北京大学出版社
PEKING UNIVERSITY PRESS

图书在版编目(CIP)数据

生动汉语百例 /李红编著；孙弢译.—北京：北京大学出版社，2011.9
(汉英对照·汉语100点实用系列手册)
ISBN 978-7-301-19516-1

Ⅰ.生… Ⅱ.① 李… ② 孙… Ⅲ.① 汉语—谚语—对外汉语教学—教学参考资料 ② 汉语—歇后语—对外汉语教学—教学参考资料 Ⅳ.H195.4

中国版本图书馆CIP数据核字(2011)第189560号

书　　名：生动汉语百例 100 Vivid Chinese Expressions
著作责任者：李　红　编著　孙　弢　译
责 任 编 辑：沈　岚
标 准 书 号：ISBN 978-7-301-19516-1/H·2939
出 版 发 行：北京大学出版社
地　　址：北京市海淀区成府路205号　100871
网　　址：http://www.pup.cn
电　　话：邮购部 62752015　发行部 62750672
　　　　　编辑部 62767349　出版部 62754962
电 子 邮 箱：zpup@pup.pku.edu.cn
印　刷　者：**北京宏伟双华印刷有限公司**
经　销　者：新华书店
　　　　　650毫米×980毫米　16开本　10.5印张　150千字
　　　　　2011年9月第1版　2011年9月第1次印刷
定　　价：36.00元(含1张MP3)

未经许可，不得以任何方式复制或抄袭本书之部分或全部内容。
版权所有，侵权必究　**举报电话：** 010-62752024
电子邮箱： fd@pup.pku.edu.cn

前 言

千里之行，始于足下。

——[中国] 老子

谚语虽短，智慧深长。

——[希腊] 索福克勒斯

众所周知，汉语谚语、歇后语和成语是人类智慧的高度结晶，人口传颂，经久不衰。它们不仅是中国人民文化和修辞的艺术宝库，而且为外国人丰富他们的思想和言语提供了取之不尽的源泉。学习外语最成功的标志就是能否熟练地掌握这些生动的语言。成功了，我们就会引起别人的注意，赢得人们的尊重和羡慕；成功了，我们就能和这种语言和文化融合在一起，成为这个社会的一员，和这个社会的人民打成一片。

在我们的中文高级班里，我们发现外国学生们都已经掌握了语法、句型，以及大量的词汇，语言的基础非常扎实。但在实际生活中，他们的语言就显得非常呆板、乏味了。尽管语法正确，这些学生仍然无法生动地表达思想感情。学习外语就好像是盖一所房子。地基（发音）有了，屋架（语法）也起来了，砖墙也砌好了。但是要想让房子优美出众，建筑风格（生动的表达方式）是必不可少的。

正是为了这个目的，我们收集了汉语里最有趣的谚语、歇后语和成语，编辑了这本《生动汉语百例》。汉语有成千上万这类的语言，我们选的是最生动、流传最广的，而且我们倾向那些能使我们浮想联翩的语句。比如，形容东西难找，我们说，大海里捞针。英文里说草垛里找针。这里的针、草垛、大海都是既简单生动又行之有效的比喻。

为了让学生恰当地应用这些词语，我们给每个条目都提供了两个长短不一的例句，以便学生体会中文语境。所有的例句都配有英文翻译，以加深对中文原意的准确理解。对词语和例句中重要的语法点和生词，我们也在小贴士中尽可能地提供一些解释。

本书是中国研究学社（China Studies Institute）中文老师们集体努力的成果。这些老师都积极参与了选择词语和提供例句的工作。中文项目的负责人肖峰更是花费了很多的时间完善注释和小贴士。没有他们的贡献，本书是无法完成的。当然，由于能力所限，书中存在的问题和错误在所难免，请各位读者不吝赐教。

既然高级班的学生已经学会了走路，我们要让他们飞跑，也许还要飞翔呢。在罗马做事要像个罗马人，在中国说话就要像个中国人。

编者

Preface

"One thousand mile journey begins with a single step."

—Lao Zi

"A short saying oft contains much wisdom."

—Sophocles

Proverbs, sayings, and idioms represent collective wisdoms in various societies, tested over the ages and among folks from all walks of life. They are a powerful cultural and linguistic treasure trove for not only the native speakers but also foreigners to find, to learn and to polish their speech. The mastery of these expressions is the ultimate litmus test for the foreign language learning. It gives us the power to command attention, respect and even admiration. It blends us immediately with the language and culture we study, bonding us as its members, rather than outsiders, and thus achieving the goal of cultural immersion.

In teaching our upper level immersion classes, we discover that students have generally achieved a solid command of Chinese grammatical structures, common patterns, and a reasonably large vocabulary. In other words, they have learned the basic essentials. To speak effectively in real life, however, is another challenge they have yet to take up. They are in dire need of something unique to express their thoughts and ideas, moving away from grammatically correct, but stylistically barren utterances. Learning a foreign language is very much like building a house. The foundation (pronunciation) is laid, the structure (grammar) put up, and the bricks (vocabulary) filled in. Yet, an architectural style (vivid expressions) has to be added to make it beautiful.

For that purpose, we have compiled a list of lively Chinese proverbs and sayings which we call Vivid Expressions. There are numerous such expressions in Chinese, but not all qualify as vivid. Our biases are set for those that are both image and thought provoking. For instance, to describe something impossible to locate, we say, "to fish for a needle out of the sea," equivalent to "to find a needle in a haystack" in English. Here, needle, haystack, and ocean are vivid metaphors, simple and effective.

In order to help students to use these expressions properly, we have provided two examples for each entry in various contexts. They are all written in Chinese, but English translations are provided for easy and precise comprehension. The grammatical principles behind these expressions and some words are also explained, to the extent possible, immediately following the examples and in a section called Tips.

This project is a collective endeavor of the language faculty at China Studies Institute, which aims to promote cultural exchange between China and America and to help American students study in China. In various ways, they have all made contributions in selecting expressions and writing up examples. Andrew Xiao, our language coordinator, spent many additional hours in perfecting explanations and providing grammar tips. Without their hard work, this book wouldn't have been possible. For the errors in the book, we sincerely appreciate suggestions and corrections.

Now that the advanced students have learned to walk, we want them to run, maybe even to fly. Do in Rome as Romans do, speak in China as Chinese speak.

目 录

A

ànbǎn shàng de ròu rèn rén zǎigē

1. 案板上的肉——任人宰割

Meat on a butcher's cutting board—to be chopped at someone's will

◈ **To be completely at other people's mercy**

歇后语，贬义。

Two-part allegorical saying, derogatory.

Examples

两个球队的实力相差太大。在比赛中A队就像案板上的肉，只能任B队宰割了。

There is a considerable gap in actual strength between the two teams. During the game, Team A was totally butchered by Team B.

A：弱小国家在国际事务中没有任何影响，都往往是案板上的肉，任人宰割。

B：我觉得你的想法有点太悲观了。

A: Weak and small nations have no influence in international affairs. They are completely at the mercy of more powerful countries.

B: I'm afraid that you are a bit over-pessimistic.

Tips

1. 像(xiàng): 动词，和……差不多一样。常用结构为：A像B，意思是A和B差不多一样。

   Verb, to be similar to; usually used in the pattern: A xiàng B, meaning A is similar to B.

2. 任(rèn)：介词，古汉语，相当于现代汉语中的“被”，表示被动，引出动作的发出者，现代汉语常用格式“A+任+B(动作的发出者)+动词”。

   Preposition, used in classical Chinese as “bèi” in modern Chinese, indicating the passive voice and introducing the doer of an act; a usual pattern is “A+ rén+B (the doer)+Verb”.

B

bā zì hái méiyǒu yì piě

2. 八字还没有一撇

Not even the first stroke of the character for eight is done.

◈ Nothing is accomplished yet.

歇后语，中性，后一句省略，用来表示事情还没有开始，不要过早想以后美好的结果。

Two-part allegorical saying, neutral, with the second part of the intended meaning unsaid or omitted; indicating that an anticipated event or result has not yet started or been realized.

Examples:

锦标赛主赛场应该今年就完工，可是现在八字还没有一撇呢。

The main stadium for the tournament should be finished by the end of this year, but so far nothing has been done yet.

A：哥本哈根环境宣言讨论得怎么样啦？

B：八字还没有一撇呢。发达国家和发展中国家还在讨价还价。

A: How is the discussion over the Copenhagen Declaration on the environment?

B: Nothing is accomplished yet. The developed and developing nations are still negotiating with each other.

Tips

1. 就(jiù)：副词，用在动词前，表示动作发生得很早或者很快。
Adverb, used before a verb to indicate that an action happened quickly or will happen soon.
2. 八(bā)：数词，数字8，汉字"八"一共两个笔画。左边第一笔叫"撇"。如果第一笔还没写，那离完成还差得很远。
Noun, eight, the Chinese character eight is consisted of two strokes, and the first is a left-falling stroke called "piě". If not even the first stroke is done, it is far from finishing up.
3. 还没有……呢(hái méiyǒu...ne)：表示动作或事件还没有发生或完成。
Denoting that an action or incident has not yet happened or finished.
4. 哥本哈根(Gēběnhāgēn)：专有名词，丹麦的首都。
Proper noun, Copenhagen, the capital of Denmark.
5. 动词+得+形容词：表示动作完成的情况或者程度。一般情况下，形容词前边要加"很"、"非常"或者"太……了"等副词或结构。疑问句形式以"怎么样"、"吗"等结尾。
Verb + de + adjective: denoting the degree of the verb/act completion; usually, words or phrases like "hěn (very)", "fēicháng (very much)", or "tài...le (too much)"; are used before the adjective. Its question form usually ends with "zěnmeyàng", "mā", etc.

bānqǐ shítou zá zìjǐ de jiǎo

3. 搬起石头砸自己的脚

To drop a rock on one's own foot

To invite trouble to oneself

◈ **A similar English expression: to shoot oneself in the foot**

谚语，贬义，表示计划对付别人的计谋没有成功，反而成了自己的麻烦。

Proverb, derogatory, meaning that one's scheme against others turns out to hurt oneself.

Examples:

房地产商不断地提高价格，一定会搬起石头砸自己的脚。

Real estate developers kept raising housing prices. As a result, they will end up shooting themselves in the foot.

A：听说有三个年轻人在动物园被老虎咬伤了。

B：是啊。他们把老虎惹急了。这就是搬起石头砸自己的脚。

A: I heard that three young men were bitten by a tiger in the zoo.

B: That's right. The tiger was provoked until it could not take it anymore. It's entirely their fault.

Tips

1. 听说(tīngshuō)：动词，也可是"听+某人+说"，常放在句子开始，表示后面的内容是听到的。
   Verb, meaning "it is said;" it also has a pattern as "tīng + somebody + shuō", meaning "it is said by somebody"; often used at the beginning of a sentence.
2. 把(bǎ)：本句中"把"字句为"A+把+B+动词+结果+(了)"，A发出了一个动作，这个动作影响了B，然后B有了一个结果。
   In the structure "A + bǎ + B + verb + result + (le)", A, a doer, takes a certain action and causes B to the result.
3. 惹(rě)：动词，古代汉语，常用格式：A惹B, B因为A做的事情生气；"A+把+B惹+结果(坏)"，B因为A得到了不好的结果。
   Verb, meaning to provoke in classical Chinese; its common patterns include: A re B (A provokes B), meaning the actions of A have offended B; "A + bǎ + B + rě + result (mostly negative)", meaning A has caused negative consequences for B.

bǎn shàng dìng dīng
4. 板上钉钉

To drive a nail into a board

◈ To have a done deal

谚语，褒义，表示事情会按计划发展，结果一定没有问题。通常用来强调对结果很有信心。

Proverb, commendatory, emphasizing confidence in that things would go smoothly and develop as planned and expected.

Examples:

合同已经签了,这个工程是板上钉[1]钉[2]了。

The contract has already been signed, and thus it's a done deal.

A: 祝贺你找到了北京的工作。

B: 我没有收到正式的通知,这事儿还不能说是板上钉钉呢。

A: Congratulations on your new job in Beijing.

B: I have not received any formal notice yet. It is not quite a done deal.

Tips

1. 钉(dìng)[1], 动词,把钉子或者其他尖锐东西打入他物,通常为起固定的作用。
   Verb, to nail a small pointed piece into other things, usually to fasten things.
2. 钉(dīng)[2]: 名词,口语中常说"钉子",一端尖锐的金属细棒;也常用于指代生活中遇到的问题等。例如,"碰钉子"意思是遇到问题和困难。
   Noun, nail, a small and thin pointed piece of metal; the same as "dīngzi" in colloquial speech; Dīngzi also is often used to indicate problems or difficulties in life, such as in "pèng dīngzi," meaning "to encounter a problem."

bèn niǎo xiān fēi
5. 笨鸟 先飞

Slow birds should make an early start.

◈ **People with less talent should start early and thus be better prepared with more time.**

成语，褒义，强调提早行动，多花时间，天赋不是很好的人也能获得很好的成绩。

Four-character idiom, commendatory, stressing that earlier start and better preparation, even from someone without the best talents, still may bring excellent achievements.

Examples:

她不是最聪明的学生，可是她笨鸟先飞，学习成绩非常棒。

She is not the brightest student, but she is always better prepared than others and has maintained an excellent academic record.

A: 你的对手非常强大，你有取胜的把握吗？

B: 笨鸟先飞吧。只要付出更多的努力，我觉得就是有希望的。

A: Your competitor is a great athlete. Can you beat him?

B: Well, being a slow bird, I plan on spending a lot more time and effort on my training, and then I will have a pretty good chance of winning.

Tips

1. 把握(bǎwò):本句中为名词,表示对事物的掌控能力;在其他情形中也可作动词,意思是控制、掌握。

   A noun in this sentence, meaning "assurance;" in other situations, also can be used as a verb, meaning to "control", or " to grasp".

2. 只要A,(就)B(zhǐyào A, (jiù) B):A是条件,B是结果;有了条件A,一定会有结果B。

   Meaning "if there is A, there will be B;" the presence of will cause the occurrence of B.

bì mén zào chē

6. 闭 门 造 车

To make a cart behind a closed door

◈ **To work on something without any firsthand knowledge or experience**

成语,贬义,表示做事脱离实际,主观臆断。

Four-character idiom, derogatory, denoting that things have been done without considering actual situation or without first-hand knowledge.

Examples:

如果你想成为杰出的演员,一定要出去观察生活。闭门造车是行不通的。

If you want to be an outstanding actor, you have to go out and observe real life. Making a cart behind closed doors will not get you very far.

A：老师留了一个作业，让我们了解老北京人的客套话。

B：你应该出去逛逛啊。闭门造车是写不出来的。

A: The teacher gave us an assignment to learn about the polite speech of traditional Beijing residents.

B: You should go out and mix with people. You'll need a lot of actual experience to understand the subject.

Tips

1. 行不通(xíng bu tōng)：做不到；否定式"动词+不+结果/趋向"表示动作不可能完成；肯定式为：动词+得+结果/趋向，例如"行得通"、"写得出来"；疑问式为：动词+得+结果/趋向+动词+不+结果/趋向，例如"行得通行不通"、"写得出来写不出来"。

Meaning "won't work"; "to be able to" its negative form "verb+bu+result /complement" indicates that an action cannot be completed; its affirmative form is "verb + de + result/complement", such as "xíng de tōng (will work)" and "xiě dechū lái(to be able to write)"; its question form is "verb + de + result/complement + verb + bu + result/complement", such as "xíng de tōng xíng bu tōng (will work or not)", or "xiě de chūlái xiě bù chūlái (to be able to write or not)".

2. 让(ràng):“让+某人+动词+宾语”表示命令或允许某人做某事。
To let; the pattern “ràng+ somebody+verb+ object” means to give an order/permission to somebody for doing something.
3. 客套话(kètàohuà):名词,用来表示客气的固定说法。
Noun, polite talk.

bǔ fēng zhuō yǐng
7. 捕 风 捉 影

To seize wind and to capture shadows

◈ **To speak or act on hearsay**

成语,贬义,表示没有根据的说法,常用来批评不实言论。
Four-character idiom, derogatory, denoting groundless statement; often used to criticize hearsays.

Examples:

一些新闻记者总是捕风捉影,报道一些没有事实根据的消息。

Some reporters are always grasping at shadows, spreading rumors as news without bothering to get their facts straight.

A: 听说你九岁时就会写诗。
B: 别信这些捕风捉影的传闻。
A: I heard you could compose poetry even at the age of nine.
B: Don't believe these baseless hearsays.

Tips

1. 报道(bàodào):动词,通过媒体把消息告诉大家。
   Verb, to report, to spread news.
2. 诗(shī):名词,一种有节奏和韵律的文学形式。
   Noun, poem.
3. 别(bié):副词,用在动词前表示"禁止"或"劝阻"。
   Adverb, used before verbs to persuade someone not to do something or to forbid someone to from doing something.

bú jiàn guāncai bú luò lèi

8. 不 见 棺材 不 落泪

No tears until seeing the coffin

◈ **Won't admit to one's mistakes until a total failure.**

谚语,贬义,意指非常固执,不到彻底失败不知道后悔和承认错误。

Proverb, derogatory, denoting one's stubbornness, not giving up a wrong course or admitting mistakes until an utter defeat.

Examples:

股票一定会大跌的,你怎么还不卖出去?真是不见棺材不落泪啊。

This stock is sure to fall. Why don't you sell it now? It will be too late otherwise.

A：他大学四年级了，怎么还玩儿游戏？现在找工作很难呀！

B：他是不见棺材不落泪。没有工作，看他怎么养活自己！

A：He is a senior at college already. How come he is still so much into playing games? You know jobs are hard to come by now.

B：He will pay for his stubbornness. Let's see how he will support himself without a job!

Tips

1. 股票(gǔpiào)：名词，占有股份的证据文件。
   Noun, stock, share.
2. 怎么(zěnme)：疑问代词，用于反问句中的动作之前，加强反问的语气。
   Question pronoun, often used in a reflexive question for emphasis.

9. 不胫而走
bú jìng ér zǒu

To walk away without legs

◈ **To spread quickly**

成语，褒义，表示好消息不用宣传，自然地很快就传开了。
Four-character idiom, commendatory, meaning that good news travels fast on its own.

Examples:

他中大奖的消息不胫而走，周围的人很快就都知道了。

He has just won the prize, and everyone soon heard about it. The news spread like a wildfire.

A：今天机场怎么有这么多的人？

B：有个著名电影明星要来的消息不胫而走，他的粉丝都很早来到这里等啦。

A: How come there are so many people at the airport today?

B: A famous movie star is supposed to come here. The news spread like crazy, and all of his fans came early to catch a glimpse of him.

Tips

1. 中(zhòng)：动词，恰好合上，如“中奖”：所抽号码与得奖号码一致。
   Verb, to attain a perfect match, to hit a target; for instance, “Zhòngjiǎng”, meaning “to win a lottery”, comes from that fact that the ticket number just matches the winner number.
2. 胫(jìng)：名词，小腿。
   Noun, a classical Chinese word, meaning “shin”, which is used as “xiǎotuǐ” instead in modern Chinese.
3. 而(ér)：连词，表示转折关系，常用于一些固定格式中，现在常用“而且”。
   Conjection, indicating transition, meaning “however”, or “but”; also often used as “érqiě”.

4. 粉丝(fěnsī)：名词，原意为大米、豆类粉等做成的丝状食品。现常用作英文“Fans”的音译，指崇拜者，热心追随者。

Noun, originally referring to noodles made of rice, potatoes, or various kinds of beans. Here it refers to admirers or passionate followers, as being a transliteration of the English word, “fans”.

bú yì ér fēi

10. 不翼而飞

To fly away without wings

◈ To disappear without a trace

成语，中性，表示东西因不明原因突然不见了。

Four-character idiom, neutral, denoting that something suddenly disappears with no reason at all.

Examples:

我刚才明明看见手机在桌子上，怎么不翼而飞了？

I did see my cell phone on the desk a moment ago. How come it disappeared without a trace?

A：你再仔细找一找那本书。它不会不翼而飞的。

B：我到处都找了，可就是找不到。

A: Keep looking for the book. It can't have walked off all by itself.

B: I've looked everywhere and still can't find it.

Tips

1. 明明(míngmíng)：副词，表示"显然这样"的意思，常常用在表示转折关系的复句中，表示事实很清楚。
   Adverb, obviously, often used in a complex sentence to denote concession.
2. 翼(yì)：名词，翅膀。
   Noun, classical Chinese, meaning "wing", often used as "chìbǎng" in modern Chinese.
3. 到处(dàochù)：副词，所有的地方，常用格式："(地点名词)+到处+都+动词……"。
   Adverb, meaning "everywhere"; a common pattern of it is: "location + dàochù + dou + verb".
4. 就(jiù)：副词，放在动词前，用来加强句子语气。
   Adverb, used before verbs for emphasis.

11. 不入虎穴，焉得虎子
bú rù hǔxué, yān dé hǔ zǐ

One cannot catch tiger's cubs without going into the tiger's den.

One must take risks to accomplish difficult tasks.

◈ A similar English expression: Nothing ventured, nothing gained.

谚语，褒义，不去冒险就不可能有想要的结果。通常用来说服别人去迎接挑战。

Proverb, commendatory, meaning that it is hard to obtain achievements without taking risks; often used to persuade others to take on challenges.

Examples:

把人质从恐怖分子的营地救出来是有危险的。但不入虎穴，焉得虎子。我们只能进去了。

It is dangerous to rescue the hostage from the terrorists' base camp but we have to take the risk. Our only option is to go in now.

A：写这方面的书要花很长时间。你真能下决心干吗？

B：不入虎穴，焉得虎子！就是花上十年，我也在所不惜。

A: To write on such a topic would take a long time. Are you sure you want to do it?

B: Nothing ventured, nothing gained. I do not mind doing it even if it would take a decade.

Tips

1. 人质(rénzhì)：名词，被强制扣留作为交换条件的无辜者。
   Noun, hostage, a victim who is held by a captor as bargaining power or security for an intended agreement.
2. 恐怖分子(kǒngbù fènzǐ)：名词，使用暴力危害社会与公众的人员。
   Noun, terrorist.
3. 焉(yān)：古汉语，疑问代词，相当于现代汉语的"怎么"。
   Question pronoun in classical Chinese, meaning "how" in modern Chinese.

4. 就是……也……(jiùshì...yě ...)："就是"的后面是一个假设，表明即使在假设的情况下，说话人也不会改变看法或认定的结果。

"jiùshì" is always followed by an assumption, indicating that even in that kind of case, the speaker will not change his or her views.

5. 在所不惜(zài suǒ bù xī)：成语，意思是"为了目标，可以牺牲一切"。

Four-character idiom, meaning "to make sacrifices without reservation in order to achieve a goal".

C

cāngying bù dīng wúfèng de dàn
12. 苍蝇不叮无缝的蛋

Flies won't sting eggs without a crack.

Events happen for a reason.

◈ **A similar English expression: Where there is smoke, there is fire.**

谚语，贬义，强调坏的影响和自身原因不能分开。

Proverb, derogatory, emphasizing that negative effect is partially caused by oneself.

Examples:

大家都相信关于他的绯闻，因为苍蝇不叮无缝的蛋。

Everyone is sure that he is involved in the scandal since there is no smoke without fire.

A：他今天在法庭上说自己是无罪的。

B：苍蝇不叮无缝的蛋。我不信他真是个干净的人。

A: He pleaded not guilty in court today.

B: Flies won't sting eggs without a crack. I do not believe he is innocent.

Tips

1. 绯闻(fēiwén):名词,本义为喜庆的事,现引申专指男女情爱的消息,中性,但因涉及敏感关系,所以常会对当事人有负面影响。
Noun, originally referring to happy events and later indicating affairs between men and women; neutral, not necessarily referring to scandals, even though it may bring negative effects to the people involved.
2. 法庭(fǎtíng):名词,审理案件的司法机构。
Noun, court, a place where lawsuits are brought to trail.

cháhú li zhǔ jiǎozi—— yǒu zuǐr dào (dào) bu chū
13. 茶壶里煮饺子——有嘴儿道(倒)不出

To cook dumplings in a teapot——unable to pour out through the mouth

◈ **Unable to express ideas or feelings**

歇后语,中性,说明因为表达能力不行,所以无法把学识展现出来。通常表示对有才能的人的一种惋惜。

A two-part allegorical saying, neutral, indicating that due to a lack of expressive ability one cannot show his or her erudition; often used to display sympathy for people in such situations.

Examples:

查理是茶壶里煮饺子——有嘴道(倒)不出。他更适合做研发而不是营销。

Charlie is knowledgeable but unable to express himself well. He is better suited for R&D than sales.

A: 那位教授的知识真是渊博,但讲课讲不出来。

B: 这就是茶壶里煮饺子——有嘴倒不出。

A: That professor is very knowledgeable, but he is not a good communicator.

B: His thoughts are like dumplings boiled in a tea pot — there's no way to get them out.

Tips

1. "道"和"倒"("dào" and "dào"):两者为同音异义字,读音相同,汉字及意思不同。
   Homophones; the first "dào", means "to pour out", while the second means "to speak out", which is actually the implied action; it is a pun.
2. 而不是(ér bú shì): 常用格式:(是)A而不是B,表示B是对的,A不对。
   Conjunction; common pattern: (shì) A érbúshì B, meaning "it is A not B".

chāi dōng qiáng bǔ　xī qiáng
14. 拆东墙补西墙

To tear down the east wall in order to repair the west wall

To resort to a makeshift resolution

◈ **A similar English expression: to rob Peter to pay Paul.**

谚语，贬义，表示紧急时刻用不成熟的方法补救，但又带来新的问题。常用来批评没有全面的考虑。

Proverb, derogatory, indicating that new problems are created while the old ones are being solved; often used to criticize people who fail to grasp the whole situation.

Examples:

你怎么能从我这儿借钱去还别人呢，这不是拆了东墙补西墙吗？

How can you borrow money from me to pay off your debts? It's like you're robbing from Peter to pay Paul.

A：咱们的进攻不够强，把后卫小张改成前锋吧。

B：不行，这是在拆东墙补西墙呢！

A: Our offense is too weak. Let's move Zhang Ming up to offense.

B: No. It would be just like taking down the east wall to mend the west wall.

Tips

1. 不是……吗？(búshì...ma?)：反问句，意思为"就是……"，常用来强调肯定语气。
Rhetorical question, meaning "it is..."; usually used to emphasize an affirmative tone.
2. 把(bǎ)：本句中把字句为"A+把+B+动词+成+C"，表示因为A发出动作，B成了C。
In the pattern "A+bǎ+B+verb+chéng+C", denoting that B becomes C because of A's action.
3. 后卫(hòuwèi)：名词，足球比赛中后场的位置或队员。
Noun, rear guard positon or rear guard.
4. 前锋(qiánfēng)：名词，足球比赛中前场的位置或队员。
Noun, advance guard position or advance guard, vanguard.

cháng zài hé biān zǒu, nǎ néng bù shī xié
15. 常 在 河 边 走，哪 能 不湿 鞋？

It is hard to avoid getting your shoes wet if you often walk by the riverside.

◆ **It is easy to get corrupted or make mistakes if temptation is always present.**

谚语，贬义，表示经常在不好的环境中自然就会受到不好的影响。通常用来说明环境对人的负面影响。
Proverb, derogatory, indicating that bad environment may have negative influences upon people.

Examples:

他本是个技艺高强的杂技演员，可是在昨天的表演中他跌倒了。真是应了那句话，“常在河边走，哪能不湿鞋”呢？

He is a very skillful acrobat. However, he fell off during his performance yesterday. Little wonder that the old saying goes, “you cannot always keep your shoes dry while often walking by the river”.

A：你知道小王因赌博被抓了吗？

B：他周围的人都不务正业。常在河边走，哪能不湿鞋？

A: Have you heard that Wang was arrested for gambling?

B: His friends are all good for nothings. Little wonder he gets into trouble.

Tips

1. 杂技演员(zájì yǎnyuán)：名词短语，表演车技、走钢丝、顶碗等技艺的专业人员。
   Noun phrase, acrobat.
2. 哪能不+动词……(呢)？(nǎ néng bù + Verb...(ne)?)：反问句，双重否定表示肯定。
   Rhetorical question; double negation to emphasize a positive tone.

3. 不务正业(bú wù zhèngyè)：成语，不做应该做的事情；常常用来批评不认真做事情的人；务，做(事情)。

Four-character idiom, not attend to one's proper duties or business; often used to criticize people who are not working hard on things as they should; wù, to do (things).

chī le qiāng yào
16. 吃了戗药

To have eaten drugs for going against others

◈ To talk in a rude and fierce manner

谚语，贬义，形容说话直接，冒犯别人。通常表示对说话人态度的不满。

Proverb, derogatory, meaning "to talk in an offensive manner"; usually used to indicate discontent with such speakers.

Examples:

大家今天千万不要跟他说话。他今天吃了戗药了，说话特冲。

We should stay away from him today. He is in a very bad mood and will go off at the slightest provocation.

A：你今天吃了戗药了吗？你说话怎么像是在训人呀？

B：对不起。今天事事都不顺，态度能好吗？

A: Why were you so rude today? You spoke as if you were scolding everybody.

B: I am sorry. With all the problems I have had today, how could I have maintained a good mood?

Tips

1. 千万(qiānwàn)：副词，表示“一定”。常常用在祈使句中。
   Adverb, meaning "must"; often used in imperative sentences.
2. 戗(qiāng)：动词，表示朝反方向，相逆，也表示(言语)冲突。
   Verb, to be against, to go against, and to clash (in words).
3. 冲(chòng)：形容词，冒犯性的直接、猛烈。
   Adjetive, aggressively direct, fierce.
4. 训(xùn)：动词，严厉地批评，常用于上级对下级，长辈对晚辈的情形。
   Verb, to scold, often used in the context that the superior talks to the junior or the elder to the younger.

chū shēng niú dú bú pà hǔ

17. 初生 牛犊不怕虎

A newborn calf is not afraid of a tiger.

◈ **Young people are not afraid of anything.**

谚语，褒义，形容年轻人敢做敢为。

Proverb, commendatory, praising young people for their courage.

Examples:

虽然是第一次参加比赛，但他初生牛犊不怕虎，以出色的表现战胜了对手。

Even though it was his first time to participate, he was not afraid and managed to win the match.

A：我儿子才十九岁，但他要竞选村长。

B：管上千口人的工作是非常不容易的。他真是初生牛犊不怕虎。

A: My son is only 19, but he wants to run for the village head.

B: It is really difficult to lead thousands of people. He is truly brave to take on such a challenge.

Tips

1. 初生牛犊(chū shēng niúdú)：名词，刚出生的小牛；小牛还没有经历过危险，不知道害怕。
   Noun, newborn calf; a newborn calf hasn't experienced any danger and thus is not afraid of anything.
2. 才(cái)：副词，本句中强调数量少，时间短。
   Adverb, emphasizing small quantity or short time.
3. 管(guǎn)：动词，管理，通过控制达到计划的目的。
   Verb, to manage, to lead (in order to achieve a certain goal).

D

dà hǎi lāo zhēn
18. 大海捞针

To fish for a needle out of the sea

To attempt an almost impossible achievement

◈ **A similar English expression: to look for a needle in a haystack.**

成语，中性，表示无法找到或很难办到。通常用来说明因为目标范围太大所以难以找到。

Four-character idiom, neutral, meaning it is impossible to find small things in a big place; often used to indicate that a task is hard to be done due to the huge span of target range.

Examples:

北京有两千万人，要想找到他，真是大海捞针呀。

Beijing has over twenty million people. Finding him will be like looking for a needle in a haystack.

A: 我相信人类迟早会找到外星人的。

B: 那是大海捞针，不容易啊。

A: I believe that sooner or later, humanity will find extra-terrestrial life.

B: That's just like trying to find a needle in a haystack.

Tips

1. 迟早(chízǎo)：副词，表示事情可能早发生，也可能晚发生，但一定会发生。
   Adverb, meaning "sooner or later", indicating that it is only a matter of time something will happen.
2. 外星人(wàixīngrén)：名词，在地球以外星球的高等动物。
   Noun, extra-terrestrial.

duì niú tán qín

19. 对牛弹琴

To play music to an ox

To go over somebody's head, or to do things in vain.

◈ **Similar English expressions: to cast pearls before swine; to talk to a brick wall.**

成语，贬义，形容完全无法理解或说话做事不看对象。

Four-character idiom, derogatory, meaning that it is not understood or that people do things without considerating the receptive ability of audiences.

Examples:

我劝老村长建立一个网站，宣传我们的土特产，但他一点儿都不懂，真是对牛弹琴。

I tried to persuade our old village leader to set up a website advertising our local products, but he had no idea what I was talking about. It felt like talking to a brick wall.

A：听说他们对牛放音乐，这样可以提高牛奶的产量。

B：真的吗？这样说来，对牛弹琴也不是完全没用的。

A: It is said that they play music to their cows so that the cows may produce more milk.

B: Really? If so, then that playing music to an ox is not totally useless.

Tips

1. 宣传(xuānchuán)：动词，为了一个目的向公众进行说明讲解传播。
   Verb, to disseminate information for a purpose; to advertise; to explain to the public.
2. 土特产(tǔtèchǎn)：名词，一个地方特有的或者著名的产品。
   Noun, local special products.
3. 一点儿都+不/没……(yìdiǎnr dōu+bù/méi...)：用来强调否定，完全否定.
   Emphasizing negative statement, as "not... at all" in English.
4. 琴(qín)：名词，一种传统的中国乐器；也用于泛指乐器，例如，钢琴、小提琴、大提琴、口琴等。
   Noun, a traditional Chinese musical instrument; often used to indicate musical instruments in general, such as gāngqín (piano), xiǎotíqín (violin), dàtíqín (cello), kǒuqín (harmonica), etc.

F

fēi é pū huǒ zì qǔ mièwáng

20. 飞蛾扑火——自取 灭亡

A moth darts into the flame—courting destruction.

◈ **To seek one's own doom**

歇后语，贬义，表示愚蠢的行为导致自我毁灭。

A two-part allegorical saying, derogatory, denoting that foolish behavior will lead to self-destruction.

Examples:

吸毒上了瘾，就像是飞蛾扑火——自取灭亡。

Drug addicts are seeking their own destruction.

A：这些海盗竟然试图拦截一艘军舰。

B：那才是飞蛾扑火——自取灭亡哪。

A: These pirates tried to attack a warship.

B: They are playing with fire.

Tips

1. 瘾(yǐn)：名词，特别深的不良爱好。

   Noun, addiction, often used to indicate an harmful and obsessive hobby.

2. 竟然(jìngrán)：副词，表示出乎意料之外，没有想到的。

   Adverb, indicating that things happen unexpectedly.

3. 拦截(lánjié):动词,中途阻挡,不让通行。
Verb, to intercept, to be obstructed halfway through.

4. 蛾(é):名词,一种很像蝴蝶但夜间活动的昆虫。
Noun, moth, a flying insect like a butterfly but mostly comes out at night.

G

gǎn yāzi shàng jià

21. 赶鸭子上架

To force a duck to get on a perch

◈ **To push someone to do something beyond his or her capability**

谚语，中性，表示让人做能力无法达到的事。通常用来推辞别人的请求或自谦。

Proverb, neutral, denoting that people cannot accomplish things beyond their abilities; mostly used to decline other's request or to show modesty.

Examples:

我是学历史的，讲城市建筑可是赶鸭子上架，太为难我了。

I am student of history. Talking about the urban architecture is something beyond my expertise.

A：大家一致选你参加歌唱比赛。

B：那怎么行？你别赶鸭子上架嘛，唱歌我可不行！

A: Everyone recommended you to participate in the singing contest.

B: What? I am a lousy singer. Please don't push me beyond my capabilities.

Tips

1. 城市建筑(chéngshì jiànzhù)：名词，城市的房屋等地表设施。
   Noun, urban architecture, including buildings and other physical structures in the city.
2. 为难(wéinán)：动词，让别人感到困难，无法应对。
   Verb, to embarrass, to make uncomfortable, to make uneasy.
3. 那怎么行?(nà zěnme xíng?)：反问句，意思是那样不行。
   Rhetorical question, meaning "it doesn't work".

gǒu jí tiào qiáng

22. 狗急跳墙

A desperate dog may jump across a wall.

People in dire circumstances may resort to extreme measures.

◈ **Similar English expressions: Despair gives courage to a coward; a cornered fox is more dangerous than a jackal.**

成语，常贬义，表示绝望中或紧急情况下会不顾一切，做事不考虑后果。

Four-character idiom, often derogatory, denoting that in despair or under emergencies people may take an extreme action regardless of consequences.

Examples:

不要太逼这个歹徒，小心他狗急跳墙，开枪伤了人质。

Let's handle this carefully and not push the gangster too hard. He may become reckless and shoot the hostages.

A：这些警察把我的车扣了。狗急了还跳墙呢。我要跟他们干到底。

B：我看不要走极端。他们也是照章办事。

A: The police seized my car. They are pushing me to the corner, and I'm going to fight them to the end.

B: Don't overdo it. After all, they were only enforcing the law.

Tips

1. 逼(bī)：动词，强迫，让别人做不愿意做的事情。
   Verb, to force, to make others to do things they don't want to.
2. 歹徒(dǎitú)：名词，破坏社会秩序，伤害他人的不良人员。
   Noun, gangster, an evil person who violates laws and brings harms to others.
3. 扣(kòu)：动词，强制将人或物留下。
   Verb, to detain, to withhold people or property through coercion.
4. 极端(jíduān)：形容词或名词，达到一个方向的极点。
   Adjective or noun, to the extreme or extreme.

6. 照章(zhào zhāng):介宾短语,根据规定。
Preposition-object phrase, in accordance with regulations.

gǒu ná hàozi duō guǎn xiánshì
23. 狗拿耗子——多管闲事

A dog catches a mouse—minding someone else's business.

◈ **To interfere with other people's business**

歇后语,贬义,表示管超出自己范围的事情。通常用来抱怨别人干涉自己的事情。

Two-part allegorical saying, derogatory, denoting getting involved in other's business; often used as a complaint.

Examples:

他不了解这里的情况,却总来对我们的计划指手画脚。完全是狗拿耗子——多管闲事。

He doesn't understand local situations here but always wants to interfere with our plans. It is totally like a dog trying to catch a mouse.

A: 请你节约用水。

B: 你别狗拿耗子,多管闲事。我不浇水,草就都死掉了。

A: Please conserve water.

B: Go mind your own business. If I don't water it, the grass will die.

Tips

1. 指手画脚(zhǐshǒuhuàjiǎo)：成语，本意为说话时手脚做动作，常指不必要的干涉。
Idiom, originally meaning to move one's hands and legs when talking, often used to indicate unwanted interference.
2. 拿(ná)：动词，用手握住或者取。
Verb, to catch, to get.
3. 耗子(hàozi)：名词，北方方言，老鼠。
Noun, rat; also known as "lǎoshǔ" in northen dialects.
4. 死掉(sǐdiào): 动词+掉，"掉"作为结果补语常常有"分开"、"分离"的意思。
In the pattern of "verb+ diào", "diào" here is used as a resultative complement, denoting separation, being parted.

gǒu zuǐ li tǔ bu chū xiàngyá
24. 狗嘴里吐不出象牙

An ivory tusk will never grow in a dog's mouth.

A mean person cannot say anything decent.

◆ **Similar English expressions: A cracked bell can never sound well; don't look for musk in dog's kennel.**

谚语，贬义，表示没教养的人说不出有教养的话。通常用来批评别人。

Proverb, derogatory, denoting that rude people cannot talk in a civil or genteel way; often used to criticize others.

Examples:

他是一个非常挑剔的人，很少看到别人的优点，评价别人的时候，也没有什么好话，狗嘴里吐不出象牙。

He's an incredibly picky person who hardly sees merits in others and says nothing nice when talking about the others.

A：小王不高兴的时候，怎么经常叫他的同事"白痴"？

B：他这人就是狗嘴里吐不出象牙。

A: How could Xiao Wang call his colleagues "idiots" in public when he is upset?

B: Well, you just cannot expect an ivory tusk from a dog's mouth.

Tips

1. 挑剔(tiāoti)：动词，过分严格地在细节上挑选。
   Verb, to select or to find fault in an unreasonable way.
2. 评价(píngjià)：动词，评论估计他人或事物的好坏。
   Verb, to evaluate, to estimate, to appraise.
3. 白痴(báichī)：名词，语言表达有问题反应迟钝的人。常用来表示对(他人的)不尊重。
   Noun, idiot, retarded; often used to show disrespect to others.

guà yáng tóu mài gǒuròu

25. 挂羊头，卖狗肉

To sell dog meat while displaying sheep head

Not to act according to promise or indication

◈ **Similar English expressions: to offer chaff for grain; to cry up wine and sell vinegar.**

谚语，贬义，表示宣传的内容和实际提供的完全不同。通常用来批评言行不一的人，或者虚假的广告。

Proverb, derogatory, denoting that the actual content is different from what was publicized; often used to criticize those people who cannot live up to their promises, or false advertisement/propaganda.

Examples:

不要相信那些伪君子。他们总是说一套做一套，挂羊头卖狗肉。

Don't trust those hypocrites. They always cry up wine but sell vinegar instead, never practicing what they preach.

A：你们是个咖啡店，怎么卖起书来了？这不是挂羊头卖狗肉吗？

B：没有办法。光卖咖啡不赚钱呀。

A: This is a coffee shop. How come you also sell books? Isn't this a case of crying up wine but selling vinegar?

B: We had no choice. It does not pay to just sell coffee.

Tips

1. 伪君子(wěijūnzǐ)：名词，表面高尚实际卑鄙的人。
   Noun, hypocrite, a person who appears to be noble but is despicable in deed.
2. 起来(qǐlái)：趋向补语，格式为“动词+起来”；如果有宾语，格式为“动词+起+宾语+来”表示动作开始并继续下去。
   Directional complement, mostly used in a pattern as “verb+qǐlái”; if there is an object, the pattern will be “verb + qí + object + lái”, denoting that the action has started and is going on.
3. 光(guāng)：副词，只，仅仅。
   Adverb, solely, only, merely.
4. 赚(zhuàn)：动词，获得利益。
   Verb, to earn, to make a profit.

guò jiē lǎoshǔ　　rén rén hǎn dǎ

26. 过街老鼠——人人喊打

A rat runs across the street—being attacked by everybody

◈ **To be hated by everyone**

歇后语，贬义，强调不道德的人会被全社会痛恨。

Two-part allegorical saying, derogatory, emphasizing that unethical people or deeds arouse public averseness and condemnation from all walks of life.

Examples:

他的贪污行为被揭露了以后，他就像过街的老鼠——人人喊打。

After his corruption was exposed, everyone took their turn denouncing him.

A：在今天的报纸上，大家对卖假奶粉的企业纷纷进行抨击。

B：这真是过街老鼠——人人喊打。

A: In today's newspapers, everyone is attacking the companies that sold fake milk powder.

B: They're like rats crossing a street — hated by everyone.

Tips

1. 贪污(tānwū)：名词，利用职权非法获得财物的行为；动词，利用职权非法获得财物。
   Noun, corruption, the abuse of the public power for personal gains; verb, to graft, to embezzle.
2. 揭露(jiēlù)：动词，把秘密的事情公布出来。
   Verb, to reveal, to expose something secret.
3. 进行(jìnxíng)：动词，指动作在进行中，常用格式是"进行+动词"。
   Verb, to be in the process of doing something; often used in the patter "Jinxing + verb".
4. 抨击(pēngjī)：动词，严厉而正式地批评。
   Verb, to denounce publicly, to condemn openly.

guò hé chāi qiáo

27. 过 河 拆 桥

To tear down the bridge after crossing it

To show ingratitude towards people who had provided help

◈ **A similar English expression: Danger past, God forgotten.**

成语，贬义，表示得到别人的帮助却不知道报答，达到目的后就把帮助过自己的人抛开。通常用来批评别人功利心太重。

Four-character idiom, derogatory, denoting that people are ungrateful and push the helper aside after achieving their goals; often used to criticize opportunists who take advantage of others and are ungrateful.

Examples:

这个歌星出名以后，再也不与过去给她很大帮助的音乐老师来往了。实在有点过河拆桥的味道。

After being famous, this singer no longer stays in touch with her previous music teacher whose help was essential for her success. It really smacks of ingratitude.

A：当初全靠我救了这个公司，可是现在他们却要解雇我。

B：这怎么行呢？他们这是过河拆桥呀。

A: Back then, I saved this company, but now they want to fire me.

B: It cannot be! They are burning the bridge after crossing it.

Tips

1. 出名(chūmíng):动词,变得有名气,广为人知。
   Verb, to become famous, to be well-known.
2. 再也不(zàiyěbù):副词,不重复(过去做过的事)。
   Adverb, no longer, no more, or not anymore.
3. 来往(láiwǎng):动词,原意为来和去,常指保持交往。
   Verb, originally meaning "to come and go", often used to indicate to have communications with, to socialize with.
4. 靠(kào):动词,相信、依赖。
   Verb, to account on, to rely on.
5. 解雇(jiěgù):动词,停止雇佣关系。
   Verb, to dismiss, to fire (an employee).
6. 这怎么行呢?(zhè zěnme xíng ne?):反问句,意思是"这不行"。
   Rhetorical question, meaning "it cannot be".

H

hǎo gāng yòng dào dāorèn shang

28. 好 钢 用 到 刀刃 上

Good steel should be saved for the blade of a knife.

◈ **The best material or people should be placed where they are put to best use.**

谚语，褒义，强调好的资源和人才要用到关键的地方。

Proverb, commendatory, emphasizing that good resources and talents should be put into best.

Examples:

他这个人当系主任有点儿屈才。好钢应该用到刀刃上，他是个当校长的好材料。

He's too good for a department chair. Good steel should be used for a knife's blade, and after all, he is prime material for a university president.

A：你挣钱很多啊，怎么什么也舍不得买呢？

B：好钢要用在刀刃上，钱要花在有用的地方。

A: You've got a well-paid job. How come you never really buy anything?

B: I'm saving the money for something more important.

Tips

1. 屈才(qū cái)：动词，才能不能充分发挥。
Verb, to do work unworthy of one's talent; cannot give full play to one's ability.
2. 钢(gāng)：名词，经过提炼不含杂质的铁。钢铁可用于比喻坚强，例如，钢铁意志。
Noun, steel, an alloy consisting mostly of iron. Gāng (steel) and tiě (iron) together can be used to indicate strength or strong, such as in "Gāngtiě yìzhì", meaning strong will.
3. 怎么……呢？(zěnme... ne?)：用来询问原因，意思是"为什么……"。
Used as an inquiry, meaning "why...."
4. 刃(rèn)：名词，刀最锋利的地方，表示重要的部分。
Noun, edge of a blade, the sharpest section, indicating a crucial part.

hǔ tóu shé wěi

29. 虎头蛇尾

A tiger's head but a snake's tail

◈ **A fine start with a poor finish**

成语，贬义，表示开始决心很大，声势很大，后来行动很小，甚至有始无终。通常用来批评做事没有持续性。

Four-character idiom, derogatory, denoting that real action cannot match with a big previous promise or high profile statement; often used to criticize people unable to carry out things in a consistent manner.

Examples:

这位作者原计划写两本书，结果只完成了几篇文章。这的确是虎头蛇尾呀。

The author originally planned to write two books, but in the end he only produced a few articles. He started with a bang and ended with a whimper.

A：我打算在新的一年里做很多事情，可是到年底的时候，真没有几件能坚持下来。

B：别自责了。大多数人的新年决心都免不了虎头蛇尾。

A: I wanted to do many things as the new year started. However, by the end of the year only few things could persist.

B: Don't be harsh on yourself. Most people's New Year resolutions are like that, starting strong but ending up much weaker.

Tips

1. 的确(díquè)：副词，表示十分肯定。
   Adverb, indeed, really; emphasizing certainty.
2. 坚持(jiānchí)：动词，保留不变。
   Verb, to persist, to insist on, to keep on without change.
3. 自责(zìzé)：动词，自己责备自己，将错误归到自己身上。
   Verb, to blame oneself, to make oneself responsible for problems.

30. 画蛇添足

huà shé tiān zú

To paint a snake and add feet onto it

To ruin a perfect effect by adding something superfluous; to act with unnecessary measures

◈ A similar English expression: to paint the lily.

成语，贬义，表示做了多余的事情。

Four-character idiom, derogatory, denoting that an action is unnecessary or redundant.

Examples:

衣服已经很漂亮，再围上这围巾，反而是画蛇添足。

The dress is beautiful as it is. Adding on such a scarf would be unnecessary.

A：我是不是应该在文章里再加几个例子？

B：没有必要。你已经有了三个很好的例子，再加就画蛇添足了。

A: Should I add more cases in the article?

B: That would be unnecessary. You already have 3 very fine cases, adding more will be just like painting the lily.

Tips

1. 围(wéi)：动词，环绕四周。
   Verb, to surround, to enclose.
2. 反而(fǎn'ér)：连词，表示跟前文意思相反或出乎意料之外，在句中起转折作用。
   Conjunction, instead; denoting that what follows is contrary to what was said before or was a result out of expectation.

huángdì de nǚ'ér bù chóu jià

31. 皇帝 的女儿不 愁 嫁

The emperor's daughter has no worry about marriage.

◈ **Highly desired people or things are assured a bright future.**

谚语，中性，强调因为有绝对的优势所以就有很大的主动性，不担心竞争。

Proverb, neutral, emphasizing that with over whelming advantages in competitions, there is no need to worry.

Examples:

你们顶尖大学的学生还担心找不到工作吗？皇帝的女儿不愁嫁呀。

Why do top university graduates like you worry about finding jobs? Just like the emperor's daughter, you will have all the offers coming to you.

A：我们这个产品节约能源，怎么到现在还没有足够的订单呀？

B：不用着急。你们是皇帝的女儿不愁嫁，迟早会打开局面的。

A: Our product is energy efficient. How come we do not have any orders?

B: Don't worry about it. The product with such good quality will sell very well.

Tips

1. 愁(chóu)：动词，为……担忧。

   Verb, to be anxious about, to worry about.

2. 能源(néngyuán)：名词，可以加工利用的一切自然资源。

   Noun, energy, power resource that people may utilize from the nature.

3. 订单(dìngdān)：名词，买东西时发给供应者的订货文书。

   Noun, order, paper sent to a provider to order goods.

4. 会……的(huì...de)：表示肯定的语气，常用来对未来的事情的肯定。

   Denoting an affirmative tone; often used to assert things that will happen in the future.

huángshǔláng gěi jī bài nián méi ān hǎoxīn
32. 黄鼠狼 给鸡拜年——没安好心

A weasel wishes "Happy New Year!" to a chicken—with evil intentions.

◈ **Someone is acting with an ill intention or ulterior motives.**

歇后语，贬义，表示表面的好意下面有不好的动机。通常用来告诫别人不能被表面的好意迷惑。

Two-part allegorical saying, derogatory, denoting evil motivation under seemingly good gestures; often used to advise others not to be fooled by superficial kindness.

Examples:

他今天突然很热情，让我觉得他是黄鼠狼给鸡拜年——没安好心。

He was unexpectedly nice with me today. I sensed that he had an ulterior motive.

A：今天上午他接到一个电话，说他中了百万大奖，但需要先交税。

B：我看那是黄鼠狼给鸡拜年，没安好心。他得小心上当。

A: This morning he got a phone call, saying he won a million dollar prize but would have to pay tax first for it.

B: The caller is up to something. He should be careful with his wallet.

Tips

1. 安(ān):动词,安装固定。
   Verb, to arrange, to plan, to install.
2. 交税(jiāo shuì):动词,按规定上交的款额。
   Verb, to pay taxes.
3. 得(děi):助动词,不得不。
   Auxiliary verb, have to.

33. 火上浇油 (huǒ shàng jiāo yóu)

To add fuel to fire

◈ **To make a situation worse**

成语,贬义,表示某一行为反而让事情恶化。通常用来劝别人别采取行动,以免让事情越来越坏。

Four-character idiom, derogatory, denoting that an action is not helping but only making things worse; often used to persuade others not to take any action in order to avoid worsening a situation.

Examples:

学生们正在抗议提高学费。如果住宿费也上涨,会火上浇油,造成恶果。

Students are already protesting against the tuition hike. Raising the housing fees would be like throwing fuel to fire. It can only make the situation worse.

A：我的博士论文到现在还没交，老师对我很不满意。

B：那你怎么还经常不去做实验？这事让你的老师知道了，那一定火上浇油，惹老师生气。

A: My dissertation is long overdue and my mentor is very upset with me.

B: Then, how come you still often miss your experiments? If your mentor knew it, it would have just made him angrier.

Tips

1. 抗议(kàngyì)：动词，强烈反对。
   Verb, to oppose strongly, to protest.
2. 恶果(èguǒ)：名词，不好的结果；恶，不好的，邪恶的；果，结果。
   Noun, bad consequence; è, bad, evil; guǒ, as in jiéguǒ, consequence.
3. 博士论文(bóshì lùnwén)：名词，获得博士学位最后必须做的研究性文章。
   Noun, doctoral dissertation, research paper for a doctoral degree.

34. 火烧眉毛 (huǒ shāo méimao)

Eyebrows on fire

◈ In the middle of a great urgency

成语，中性，强调事情非常紧迫。

Four-character idiom, neutral, emphasizing the urgency of a situation.

Examples:

展会马上就要开始了，展品怎么还没送到？真是火烧眉毛呀。

The exhibition will open very soon. How come the items have not been delivered yet? We need them here urgently.

A：中国学校快要开学了，可我还没收到签证。这真是火烧眉毛啊。

B：不用着急，说不定明天就来了。

A: The new semester in China is going to start soon, but I haven't gotten my visa yet. I need it urgently.

B: Relax, maybe it will arrive tomorrow.

Tips

1. 展会(zhǎnhuì)：名词，展示产品科技等的集会。
   Noun, exhibition fair.
2. 要……了(yào...le)：表示一个情况就要变化或新情况很快就要发生。"要"的前边还可以加上"就"或"快"，表示时间紧迫。
   Denoting that things will change or a new situation will occur soon. "jiù" or "kuài" can be placed before "yào" to indicate time urgency.

3. 签证(qiānzhèng)：名词，国家允许外国公民出入境或过境的证明。签，签字，签名；证，证书，证明。

Noun, visa, a document issued by a country giving permission to foreigners to enter or pass through the country. Qiān, to sign, to sign name; zhèng, certificate, proof.

J

jīdàn pèng shítou

35. 鸡蛋 碰 石头

To hit a stone with an egg

◈ **To challenge the strong or powerful from a weak position or with minor force**

歇后语，贬义，后一句省略，形容双方实力差太多，所以一方必定失败。通常用来劝别人要对自身有正确的评价，别做无意义的挑战。

Two-part allegorical saying, derogatory, with the second part of the intended meaning unsaid; denoting one side is doomed due to imbalanced strength; often used to persuade people not to take on any hopeless challenges.

Examples:

他是总经理，你和他争论是鸡蛋碰石头，没什么好结果。

He is the general manager. Arguing with him will be like hitting stone with an egg, with no chance of success.

A：那个国家不大，可他们的外交很是强硬，经常向大国强国挑战。

B：我觉得他们是鸡蛋碰石头，很不明智。

A: That nation is small but their foreign policy is really tough. They always dare to provoke some big and strong nations.

B: I don't think it is a wise policy; it's like hitting a rock with eggs.

Tips

1. 争论(zhēnglùn)：动词，因意见不同进行的激烈讨论。
   Verb, to argue, to dispute.
2. 挑战(tiǎozhàn)：动词，主动出击；名词，刺激性的任务或者困难。
   Verb, to challenge; noun, challenge.
3. 明智(míngzhì)：形容词，反应快，判断准确。
   Adjective, shrewd, prudent, wise.

jiǎn le zhīma diū le xīguā

36. 捡了芝麻 丢了西瓜

To have gained a sesame but lost a watermelon

To lose something big for a small gain

◈ A similar English expression: Penny wise and pound foolish

谚语，贬义，表示注意了小的方面，却忽视了大的方面。
Proverb, derogatory, meaning that important issues are neglected as the attention is paid to trivial problems.

Examples:

他为了省一百块钱打的费，坐公共汽车去机场，结果误了飞机。真是捡了芝麻丢了西瓜！

In order to save a hundred dollars, he took a bus to the airport instead of a taxi, and missed his flight as a result. He saved small, but lost big!

A：我这次考试又失败了。

B：别再花很多时间去乐队练习，耽误学习了。这是捡了芝麻丢了西瓜！

A: I failed the exam again.

B: Don't neglect your school work in order to spend more time practicing with your band. It is penny wise and pound foolish!

Tips

1. 为了(wèile)：介词，引出目的或受益者。
   Preposition, indicating purpose; the same as "for."
2. 打的(dǎ dī)：动宾短语，源于广东方言中的"搭的士"，指坐出租车。后简化为常用口语"打的"。
   Verb-object phrase, to take a taxi, originated from "dǎ dīshì", a Guangdong dialect, where taxi is called "dīshì". Later it is simplified as "dǎ dī" and used nationwide.
3. "又"和"再"都可以表示行为或动作的重复。"再"只能用于将要出现的行为和动作，"又"可以用于已经发生或正在进行的行为或动作。
   "yòu" and "zài" both indicate repeat of action or a deed. However, "zài" is only used

when the repeated action or deed will occur in the future, while "yòu" is used to indicate the repeat that already took place or is in process.

4. 耽误(dānwù)：动词，即因拖延或错过时机而没能做某事。"耽"为拖延，"误"为错过。

Verb, meaning that something is not done due to delay or opportunity missed. "Dān" means "to delay", and "wù" means "to miss".

jià jī suí jī (jiào), jià gǒu suí gǒu (tiào)

37. 嫁鸡随鸡(叫)，嫁狗随狗(跳)

To crow with a rooster if married to a rooster, to run with a dog if married to a dog

◈ **To stay in a marriage no matter if it is beneficial, or to be totally submissive to the husband no matter what.**

谚语，贬义，形容完全顺从，虽然对现状不满，但也放弃了改变的思想。常用来表达个人对婚姻、事业的不满和无奈。

Proverb, derogatory, describing that people are totally submissive, with no desire to make any change in spite of discontent with a given situation; often used to indicate people's dissatisfaction yet lack of courage for a change.

Examples:

当今中国社会很多女人都非常有主见，比较独立，不再是嫁鸡随鸡，嫁狗随狗。

In today's China many women have their own ideas and views and are quite independent, no longer being totally submissive to their husband.

A：听说你丈夫要去外地工作了，这么说，你也得离开这儿了？

B：唉，没办法，嫁鸡随鸡，嫁狗随狗嘛！

A: I hear your husband will work in another place. In this case, are you leaving too?

B: Yes, I have no other choice, as our old saying goes, if married to a rooster, you have to crow with the rooster.

Tips

1. 主见(zhǔjiàn)：名词，自己对事物的看法和认识。
   Noun, one's own ideas and views.
2. 独立(dúlì)：形容词，不依靠别人的。也常用做动词，单独站立。
   Adjective, independent, on one's own; also often used as a verb, to stand alone, to be on its own.
3. 不再(búzài)：副词，不重复，不像过去那样。
   Adverb, no longer, not any more.

4. 嫁(jià)：动词，女子结婚。常与"给"连用，嫁给。与"娶"相对，娶指男子结婚。
Verb, to marry (for women only). By the Chinese tradition, Jià is used when women marry men, and it is often followed by "gěi" as in Jiàgěi, meaning to be married to, while for men "qǔ" is used, meaning to marry.

jiāngshān yì gǎi běnxìng nán yí
38. 江山易改，本性难移

It is easier to remove mountains and rivers than to change people's nature.

People will not change easily.

◈ **Similar English expressions: A fox may grow grey, but never good. A leopard never changes its spots.**

谚语，贬义，强调本性是无法彻底改变的。通常用来评价人的性格。
Proverb, derogatory, emphasizing the difficulties to change one's nature; often used to criticize one's character.

Examples:

他怎么又开始到处吹牛啊？真是江山易改，本性难移。
Look! He is off bragging again. I guess old habits die hard.

A：几十年没见了，可是脾气性格还跟年轻的时候一模一样。
B：是啊，江山易改，本性难移啊。

A: I haven't seen him for decades, and he still acts the same as when he was young.
B: Yeah, a leopard never changes its spots.

Tips

1. 吹牛(chuī niú):动词,说大话。
   Verb, to brag; to make exaggerated and empty talks.
2. 脾气(píqi):名词,人的性情。
   Noun, temperament.
3. 跟……一模一样(gēn... yì mú yí yàng):形容完全相同,没有什么两样。
   Meaning exactly the same, with no difference at all.

jiǎo cǎi liǎngzhī chuán

39. 脚 踩 两 只 船

With feet in two boats

To have a divided mind

◈ **A similar English expression: to sit on the fence.**

谚语,贬义,表示同时与两方保持紧密关系。通常用来批评缺乏忠诚。

Proverb, derogatory, denoting that to have relations with two sides at the same time; often used to criticize people's lack of fidelity in relationships.

Examples:

安娜有两个男朋友。她不能脚踩两只船，必须要做一个选择。

Anna is seeing two guys at the same time. She cannot be indecisive and must make a choice between them.

A：玛丽已经跟一家公司签了合同了，可是今天她又去另一家公司面试了。

B：她这不是脚踩两只船吗？

A: Mary has already signed a contract with one company, but she still went for an interview with another one today.

B: It sounds like she has her feet in two boats.

Tips

1. 踩(cǎi)：动词，用脚放在别的东西的上面。
   Verb, to step on.
2. 合同(hétong)：名词，双方或多方明确各自权利和义务的书面文件。
   Noun, contract, legally binding agreement between two or more parities with specified rights and obligations.
3. 面试(miànshì)：名词；面，面对面；试，考试；面对面的考试，主要通过口头的问答完成。
   Noun, interview; miàn, face, face to face; shì, test, exam; indicating a text or an exam that is done face to face, mostly through conversations.

jiǎo tù sān kū
40. 狡兔三窟

A cunning rabbit has three burrows.

A clever person has more than one hideout.

◈ **A similar English expression: the mouse that has but one hole is quickly taken.**

成语，中性，表示事先就有了多种应变的计划。

Four-character idiom, neutral, denoting that multiple plans are made before hand.

Examples:

那些毒贩是狡兔三窟，警察还没有找到他们。

Those drug dealers have several hideouts, so that the police haven't found them yet.

A：我想再买一套住房。

B：你都有两套房子了，再买一套，那正好是狡兔三窟呀。

A: I was hoping to buy another apartment.

B: You have two already. With one more in hands, then you truly will become "a cunning rabbit".

Tips

1. 毒贩(dúfàn)：名词，贩卖毒品的人。
   Noun, drug dealer.
2. 狡兔(jiǎo tù)：名词，狡猾的兔子。狡，狡猾，不老实，多诡计。
   Noun, cunning rabbit, foxy rabbit. (Jiǎo), cunning, crafty, sly, with many tricks.

3. 窟(kū)：名词，洞穴；人聚集的地方，多指歹徒聚集之所。
Noun, hole, cave; also used for places where people come together, especially where gangsters get together.

jìn shuǐlóu tái xiān dé yuè
41. 近水楼台先得月

The pavilion nearest the water gets a reflection of moon first.

◈ **Geographical or social advantages bring in good opportunities.**

成语，中性，表示离得近，关系近或熟悉，所以更容易得到想要的东西。通常用来解释一个结果的出现是理所当然的。
Four-character idioms, neutral, denoting that someone or something has advantages or privileges to obtain what they want; often used to indicate a result coming from easy accesses.

Examples:

这个餐馆旁边就是水库。所以，他们近水楼台先得月，总有新鲜的活鱼。
This restaurant is right next to a reservoir so it always has fresh fish.

A：听说他赢得了今年武术比赛的冠军。
B：是啊。他来自武术世家。近水楼台先得月嘛。

A: I heard that he won the championship in this year's martial arts competition.

B: Yes, he did. He is from a martial arts family and he got a better jump start than others.

Tips

1. 水库(shuǐkù)：名词，人造蓄水区域。库，储存东西的房子或地方，如粮库、国库、宝库。
   Noun, reservoir, a project to store water; kù, storehouse, warehouse, such as in liángkù (grain storehouse), guókù (national treasury), and bǎokù(treasure house).
2. 武术(wǔshù)：名词，打拳或使用传统兵器(如棍棒刀剑等)的技术。
   Noun, martial arts, the fighting arts or skills of boxing, swordplay, or using other traditional weapons such as cudgel and knife.
3. 世家(shìjiā)：名词，有地位和传统的家族。
   Noun, a big family with long traditions.

jǐng dǐ zhī wā

42. 井 底 之 蛙

A frog at the bottom of a well

◈ **A person who holds narrow views**

成语，贬义，表示看得不远，思维很狭隘。通常用来批评别人没有全局观。

Four-character idiom, derogatory, denoting short-sightedness and narrow-mindedness; often used to criticize people who cannot see a whole picture.

Examples:

我以为中国非常贫穷落后，可到了北京才知道自己真是井底之蛙。

I thought China was poor and backward and did not realize how ignorant I was until I came to Beijing.

A：他上周作文比赛得了全校第一，然后到处跟人吹自己的水平。

B：他就是井底之蛙，没见过世界有多大呀。

A: He took first place in the school's essay contest last week and has been bragging about it since.

B: He is really a frog in a small well, not knowing how big the outside world is.

Tips

1. 贫穷(pínqióng)：形容词，钱财不足，缺乏物质财产。
   Adjective, poor, impoverished.
2. 落后(luòhòu)：形容词，发展水平比较低，或者不如别人。
   Adjective, backward, under-developed.
3. 之(zhī)：古汉语词，现代汉语中，常可以当"名词/形容词+的+名词"中"的"来解释。
   Classical Chinese, equivalent to "de" in modern Chinese as in "noun/adjective+de+noun".

jǐng shuǐ bú fàn hé shuǐ

43. 井水不犯河水

Water from a well won't interfere with water from a river.

◈ **One should not poke one's nose into other's affairs.**

谚语，中性，表示互不干涉就没有矛盾。通常用于敌对双方的警告。

Proverb, neutral, denoting that there will be no conflict if there is no interference; often used as a warning.

Examples:

他俩虽然很敌对，但井水不犯河水，同住一栋楼却相安无事。

Although they had a feud between them, by adopting the policy of non-interference, they live in the same building without a problem.

A：咱们早就说好了，井水不犯河水。你干吗插手我的事情？

B：没有啊，我只是想给你提些建议。

A: We agreed not to interfere with each other. Why are you poking your nose in my business?

B: I'm not. I only meant to make some suggestions.

Tips

1. 敌对(díduì)：形容词，把别人看成自己的敌人。
   Adjective, hostile, treating others as enemies
2. 犯(fàn)：动词，违反规定；做不好的事情，比如犯罪、犯法。

Verb, to offend, to violate; to do bad things, such as in fànzuì (to commit a crime) and fànfǎ (to violate a law).

3. 相安无事(xiāng'ān wú shì)：成语，彼此相处没有什么争执或冲突，还过得去。
Four-character idiom, no argument or conflicts with each other.

4. 干吗(gàn má)：口语词汇，用来询问原因，表示为什么。
Colloquial, used to ask for a reason, meaning "why".

5. 插手(chā shǒu)：动词，强行参与别人的事情；插，插入。插手，将手放入别人的事情中。
Verb, to intervene (others' affairs). Chā, to insert, to put into; chāshǒu literarily means to put one's hand into (others' business).

44. 九牛二虎之力
jiǔ niú èr hǔ zhī lì

The strength of nine bulls and two tigers

The maximum amount of effort

◈ **Similar English expression: Herculean efforts; one's utter most.**

成语，中性，强调尽了最大的努力。通常用来说明办事过程非常艰辛，成果很不容易得到。

Idiom, neutral, emphasizing enormous efforts; often used to denote that achievements are accomplished after overcoming difficulties.

Examples:

我们费了九牛二虎之力爬到山顶去拍照，结果发现忘了带照相机。

Having exhausted ourselves, we climbed to the top of the mountain for pictures, but only to find out that we had forgot to bring the camera.

A：习惯语词典编得怎么样了？

B：我们费了九牛二虎之力，才搞好了五十个条目。

A: Where are you in compiling the dictionary of idioms and expressions?

B: We did our utter most but found that we had only completed 50 entries.

Tips

1. 费(fèi)：动词，花费、耗费，常用“费力”、“费功夫”、“费时间”等。
   Verb, to spend, to cost; often goes with other words such as “fèilì”, “fèi gōngfu”, “fèi shíjiān”, etc.
2. 爬(pá)：动词，原意为贴着地面前行；常指向上走。
   Verb, to crawl, to creep; often used as to climb, to move upward.

jiǔ xiāng bú pà xiàngzi shēn

45. 酒香 不怕 巷 子 深

Good wine still enjoys high reputation even if sold in a deep alley.

A good product, or an institution, attracts people by its fame not by its location.

◈ A similar English expression: Good wine needs no bush.

谚语，褒义，强调好东西或优秀的人才不需要宣传就能得到大家的认可。

Proverb, commendatory, emphasizing that no promotion or propaganda is needed for excellent goods or talents.

Examples:

虽然说酒香不怕巷子深，可是现在就业市场竞争激烈。一个人必须推销自己，否则找不到好的工作。

Although good wine needs no push, the competition in today's job market is fierce. One has to advertise himself to the world to get a good job.

A：你为什么不在电视上做广告呢？

B：酒香不怕巷子深，只要我们的产品质量好，不怕没人买。

A: Why don't you buy some air time on TV and put up a commercial?

B: We have great products, so that the marketing will be easy as long as we maintain high quality.

Tips

1. 巷子(xiàngzi)：名词，城市中的小街道。

   Noun, a small alley, a narrow street in the city.

2. 竞争(jìngzhēng)：名词，争夺，比赛；也作动词，为了一个目标和别人争夺。

   Noun, competition, emulation. Also often used as a verb, to compete, to vie for .

3. 推销(tuīxiāo)：动词，原指推广货物的销路，引申为采用自我推荐的方法让别人认可并接纳自己。

   Verb, originally meaning to promote goods; implying to promote oneself by self-introduction.

K

kāi mén jiàn shān　yǒu huà zhí shuō

46. 开门见山——有话直说

Open the door to see the mountain

To speak one's mind in a straight forward manner

成语，中性，表示说话直接。通常用来开始一段直接的表达。

Four-character idiom, neutral; denoting straight talk; often used at the beginning of a direct statement.

Examples:

他谈生意喜欢开门见山，很少拐弯抹角。

He is often direct in business matters and rarely beat around the bush.

A：你想说什么，就开门见山地说吧。

B：我们的种树计划需要大量捐款。您能支持一下吗？

A: If you've got something on your mind, then lay it out on the table.

B: Our tree planting program needs a lot of donations. Could you help us out some?

Tips

1. 谈生意(tán shēngyi)：口语，做生意。

   Colloquial, to do business.

2. 拐弯抹角(guǎi wān mò jiǎo)：成语，不直接说出来。

   Four-character idiom; don't say things directly but beat around the bush.

3. 捐款(juān kuǎn)：名词，免费拿出来帮助别人的钱；也可作动词，免费拿钱帮助别人。

   Noun, donation in cash may; also used as a verb, to donate money.

4. 能……吗？(néng...ma?)：常用来表示请求，问别人或者自己是否可以做某事。

   Often used to indicate a request, asking if others or oneself may do something.

L

làiháma xiǎng chī tiān'é ròu

47. 癞蛤蟆 想 吃天鹅 肉

A toad wants to eat swan meat.

◈ **People desire the impossible.**

谚语，贬义，形容过高估计了自己的能力，设定的目标根本不能实现。通常用来讽刺喜欢过高估计自己能力的人。

Proverb, derogatory; denoting that people over-estimate themselves and want to gain impossible achievements; often used to mock people for their over-estimation of their abilities.

Examples:

你第一次拍电影就想拿大奖，不觉得是癞蛤蟆想吃天鹅肉吗？

This is only your first movie, yet you want to get the top prize. Don't you think it's like a toad desiring to eat swan meat?

A：王先生想娶电视台的主持人，你知道吗？

B：什么？就他那性格和能力？真是癞蛤蟆想吃天鹅肉。

A: Do you know that Mr. Wang wants to marry the news anchor?

B: What? A guy like him with no talent or personality? He must be daydreaming.

Tips

1. 电视台(diànshìtái)：名词，播放电视节目的地方。
   Noun, TV station.
2. 主持人(zhǔchírén)：名词，主持电视节目的人。
   Noun, host, TV anchor.

lǎo mǎ shí tú

48. 老马识途

An old horse always knows the way.

◈ **Experienced people can solve problems more easily.**

成语，褒义，表示有经验的人做事可靠。通常用来肯定经验的重要性。

Four-character idiom, denoting that experienced people are reliable; often used to indicate the importance of experience.

Examples:

要想让我们的企业起死回生，还真得请回老厂长，还是老马识途啊！

In order to revive our company, we should bring back our old manager. After all, we believe the old horse always knows the way.

A：不知道这件事交给老李去做合适不合适。

B：我觉得他是最好的人选。俗话说"老马识途"，他在这个行业已经工作几十年了，没有问题。

A: I don't know if Old Li is the best person for the job?

B: I think he is the best choice. As a veteran in this field, there should be no problems for him.

Tips

1. 起死回生(qǐ sǐ huí shēng)：成语，原指把快要死的人救活。常指将没有希望的事挽救过来。
Idiom, originally meaning to bring a dying person back to life. Often used to indicate to save or change a hopeless situation.

2. 人选(rénxuǎn)：名词，为了一个目标而准备考虑的备选者。
Noun, candidate pool, a group of people who are considered suitable for something.

3. 俗话说(súhuàshuō)：根据通俗的说法或当地的习惯说法。
As the saying goes.

lín zhèn mó qiāng

49. 临阵 磨枪

To sharpen the spear right before the battle

◈ **To make preparations at the last moment**

成语，贬义，表示临时开始准备，没有足够的时间准备好。通常用于批评别人没有计划性。

Four-character idiom, derogatory; denoting preparation in a hurry; often used to criticize people having no plans before hand.

Examples:

今年的比赛很重要。我们一定要好好准备，不能临阵磨枪。

This year's competition is very important. We had better prepare beforehand instead of a last minute rush.

A：明天就要考试了，你怎么现在才开始复习？
B：临阵磨枪，不快也光嘛。看看还是比不看好。

A: Our test is tomorrow. How come you just started reviewing?
B: I know it won't do much good, but cramming at the last minute is still better than doing nothing at all.

Tips

1. 磨(mó)：动词，打磨，抛光。
   Verb, to grind, to sharpen, to polish.
2. 不快也光(bú kuài yě guāng)：虽然不很锋利（"快"指锋利），但至少比较光亮；准备不好比没准备好。
   Although it won't be sharp, it at least will be shiny; denoting that not-so-good preparation is better than no preparation.

liú dé qīngshān zài bù pà méi chái shāo

50. 留得 青山 在，不怕 没 柴 烧

If the green mountain is still there, there will be no shortage of firewood.

◈ **A similar English expression: When there is life, there is hope.**

谚语，褒义，要保存实力，等待机会再发挥。通常用来安慰别人耐心等待以后的发展。

Proverb, commendatory, meaning that people should save their strength for later development; often used to persuade others to be patient for a better future.

Examples:

这次地震毁坏了我们所有的房子，但没有摧毁我们的生命和意志。留得青山在，不怕没柴烧。我们一定会重建我们的家园。

This earthquake has ruined all of our houses but not our lives and wills, by which we will build up our home again for sure.

A: 看来因为这场暴风雪我们不能攀登珠穆朗玛峰了。为了避免伤亡，我建议立即返回大本营。

B: 同意。我们应该保存实力。留得青山在，不怕没柴烧。将来还会有机会的。

A: It seems that due to this snow storm we cannot keep climbing the Mt. Everest. My suggestion is to return to the base camp immediately in order to avoid injuries and even deaths.

B: Agree. We should save our energy and strength. With our whole team intact, we will have chance in the future.

Tips

1. 毁坏(huǐhuài):动词,破坏,损害。
   Verb, to ruin, to damage.
2. 摧毁(cuīhuǐ):动词,破坏,毁坏。
   Verb, to ruin, to destroy.
3. 青山(qīngshān):名词,因树木众多而颜色很绿的山。
   Noun, green hills with many trees.
4. 柴(chái):名词,烧火用的草木。过去人们大多从树木众多的山里拣柴。
   Noun, firewood. In the past, people mostly could pick up their firewood from the mountains with many trees. Thus, green hills are regarded as an everlasting source of firewoods.
5. 暴风雪(bàofēngxuě):名词,伴有狂风的大雪天气。
   Noun, snowstorm, blizzard.
6. 珠穆朗玛峰(Zhūmùlǎngmǎfēng):专有名词,世界第一高峰。
   Proper noun, the Mt. Everest, the highest mountain in the world.
7. 避免(bìmiǎn):动词,防止,使某情形不发生。
   Verb, to prevent, to avoid, to shun from.
8. 大本营(dàběnyíng):名词,据点的所在地。
   Noun, base camp, or stronghold.

lǘ chún bù duì mǎ zuǐ

51. 驴唇 不对马嘴

The lips of a donkey do not fit the mouth of a horse.

◈ **Not compatible or relevant**

谚语，贬义，强调说的或做的和要求完全不一样。

Proverb, derogatory, emphasizing that one's deeds doesn't match requirements at all.

Examples:

他上课没有认真听讲，所以回答问题时说得驴唇不对马嘴的。

He never paid attention in class. When he was called to respond, he could not give a relevant answer.

A：你翻译的和原文都不一样，简直是驴唇不对马嘴。

B：对不起，我只干了半年的翻译。

A: Your translation does not match the original text, the two are completely incompatible.

B: I'm sorry I have only been a translator for half a year.

Tips

1. 对(dùi):动词,合适,使相合。
   Verb, to fit, to match with.
2. 简直(jiǎnzhí):程度副词,说话人常用这个词来突出自己的观点或态度,即事物或状态达到的程度非常高,相当于"很"、"十分"。
   Degree adverb, meaning "simply", "very much"; often used to emphasize one's opinion or view.

M

miào xiǎo róng bù dé dà púsà

52. 庙 小 容 不得 大菩萨

A small temple cannot accommodate a big Buddha.

A minor institution cannot handle great talents.

◈ A similar English expression: big fish in a small pond

谚语，中性，表示一个机构不能留住人才。通常用来表达一种无奈。

Proverb, neutral, denoting that an organization or institution cannot keep talents; often used to show one's helplessness in such a situation.

Examples:

咱们公司庙太小，容不得他这个大菩萨。他注定是要去大公司的。

Our company was too small for a person of his caliber. He is bound for a much bigger firm.

A：听说你们教练跳到别的队了。

B：是啊，咱们队是庙小容不得大菩萨。

A: I hear that your coach is now with another team.

B: Yes, our pond is too small for such a big fish like him.

Tips

1. 庙(miào): 供奉神佛祖先或者历史名人的地方，例如祖庙、孔庙、寺庙。
   Noun, temple, shrine, a place where people worship gods, Buddha, ancestors or famous people, such as in zǔmiào (ancestral temple), kǒngmiào (Confucius temple), and sìmiào (Buddhist temple).
2. 容不得(róng bu dé)：可能补语，动词+不+得，表示不赞同。原指空间有限。
   Possibility complement, verb + bu + dé, indicating disapproval or preventing things happening; originally indicating a lack of space.
3. 注定(zhùdìng)：副词，预先决定，不可避免。
   Adverb, to be fated or destined.
4. 跳(tiào)：动词，从一处到另一处。也作跳槽，原指牲口离开所在的槽头到别的槽头去吃食，现在常用来比喻人离开原来的工作，另谋高就。
   Verb, to jump, to hop; also used as tiàocáo, originally denoting that livestocks switch to a different feeder, now often used to indicate hopping to a different job.

N

ná zhe jīmáo dāng lìngjiàn

53. 拿着 鸡毛 当 令箭

To take a chicken feather as a token of authority

To treat a worthless item like a command from higher up

◈ **To abuse one's power**

谚语，贬义，以权势者的言论作为行动的根据。强调过分夸大的权力，得不到服从与认可。

Proverb, derogatory; meaning to act by the authority of other powers, and that overstated authority gains no willing obedience.

Examples:

老板不在的时候，会让助理负责一下，那个助理就对大家呼来喊去的，真是拿着鸡毛当令箭！

When our boss is out, his assistant might be put in charge for something, then that assistant would order people around. It is just like taking a chicken feather as a token of authority!

A：校长要求所有的学生打预防针，咱们赶紧做准备吧。

B：你别拿着鸡毛当令箭。那只是他个人的意见而已。

A: Our principal wants every student to get vaccinated. Let's hurry up and get ready for it.

B: Don't take a chicken feather as a token of authority. That was only his personal opinion, expressed rather casually too.

Tips

1. 令箭(lìngjiàn):名词，古代军中传令用的小旗，竿头有箭头。

   Noun, small flag with an arrow on top indicating military order in ancient times.

2. 预防针(yùfángzhēn):名词，预防疾病的针剂注射;预防，预防疾病;针，针剂。

   Noun, preventive injection, vaccine; yùfáng, prevention, or to prevent (disease); zhēn, needle, needle shot.

3. 赶紧(gǎnjǐn):副词，加快速度做事。

   Adverb, hurriedly.

4. 而已(éryǐ):助词，用在陈述句末尾，有把事情往小里说的意味。常与"不过"、"无非"、"只"、"仅仅"等呼应。

   Particle, meaning "that's all" or "merely"; used at the end of sentences to downplay the significance of a statement; often cooperate with words such as "búguó", "wúfēi", "zhǐ", "jǐnjǐn", etc.

54. 泥菩萨过江——自身难保

ní púsà guò jiāng　zìshēn nán bǎo

A clay Buddha crosses a river—hardly being able to save itself.

◈ **People who cannot protect themselves have no ability to help others.**

歇后语，中性，表示在危机中自身都很难保证不受影响，就不要再想帮别人了。通常劝别人先保住自己，再想办法救别人。

Two-part allegorical saying, neutral, denoting that when it is hard to save oneself, it is not possible to help others; often used to persuade others to help themselves first before helping others.

Examples:

现在经济危机这么严重，连那家大公司都泥菩萨过江——自身难保了。

The current economic crisis is so severe that even that big company can barely save itself, just like a clay Buddha crossing a river.

A：明天是最后的期限了，但我做不完。能帮帮忙吗？

B：真是对不起。我是泥菩萨过江——自身难保。

A: Tomorrow will be the deadline for my project, but I cannot finish it. Could you give me a hand?

B: sorry. I am also in trouble and can hardly handle my own workload as it is.

Tips

1. 连 + 某 人/某 事 + 都 ……(lián + somebody/something+dōu...)：某人/某事 表示最不可能的事已经发生，通常用来暗示其他更加可能的事情一定会发生。

Denoting that an unlikely event had happened; often used to infer that a more probable event is bound to follow.

O

ǒu duàn sī lián

55. 藕断 丝连

Broken lotus roots are still connected by filaments.

◈ **To remain connected covertly after separation**

成语，中性，强调不能彻底分开。通常用来表达关系密切，不能分离。

Four-character idiom, neutral, denoting there is no thorough separation; often used to indicate remained connection due to previous closeness.

Examples:

怎么她最近还常来找你？难道你们还藕断丝连吗？

Why did she come to see you so often lately? Are you two still holding out for each other?

A：虽然他们移民到了新的国家，但他们和原来的文化藕断丝连，依然保持着密切的关系。

B：那当然啦。他们是在原来国家的文化里长大的嘛。

A: They have migrated to a new country. However, they are deeply bound up with their original culture.

B: Of course they are, as they grew up in that cultural environment.

Tips

1. 难道(nándào)：副词，用在反问句的句首，或者加强反问的语气。

   Adverb, emphasizing the rhetorical tone.

2. 藕(ǒu)：名词，莲花的根。

   Noun, lotus roots.

3. 依然(yīrán)：副词，和过去的情况一样。

   Adverb，as usual, still.

P

pífú hàn shù bú zì liàng lì

56. 蚍蜉撼树——不自量力

Ants shake a tree—not understanding their own strength.

◈ **Overestimating one's abilities**

歇后语，贬义，表示因为弱小而无法竞争。通常用来劝他人要谨慎，别做自己能力不及的挑战。

Two-part allegorical saying, denoting that the weak cannot compete with the strong; often used to persuade others to be cautious, not to take on a challenge beyond one's capacity.

Examples:

民主是历史的必然。谁要想阻挡民主的发展，只能是蚍蜉撼树——不自量力。

Democracy is a historical certainty. Whoever wants to resist such a development is fighting against the inevitable.

A：美国有个人不满政府的税收制度，驾着飞机撞了当地的税务局。

B：他这是蚍蜉撼大树，不自量力。这样做就能改变政策吗？

A: An American who was upset about the tax system flew his airplane into a local IRS building.

B: He overestimated his influence. Do you think he can change the policy by doing this?

Tips

1. 蚍蜉(pífú): 名词，古代汉语，蚂蚁。
   Noun, classical Chinese, ant.
2. 撼(hàn): 动词，摇动。
   Verb, to shake.
3. 税收制度(shuìshōu zhìdù): 名词短语，关于纳税的具体规定。
   Noun phrase, tax system.

pí xiào ròu bú xiào

57 皮笑肉不笑

A smile that is only skin deep

To make a fake, insincere smile

成语，贬义，形容笑得很虚假，或者没有善意。通常用来指出内心的阴险。

Four-character idiom, derogatory, describing hypocritical smile or kindness without sincerity; often used to denote superficial kindness with intended treachery.

Examples:

看他那张皮笑肉不笑的脸！我真是不能信任他。

Look at his superficial smiles! I really cannot trust him.

A：这个剧里，最难演的就是这个坏人皮笑肉不笑的表情。

B：您放心。我一定把他演得活灵活现。让观众体会到他的虚伪。

A: This villain is the main character in the play, and the most difficult thing to portray is the villain's false smile.

B: Don't worry about it. I'll bring the character to life and let the audience see his hypocrisy.

Tips

1. 信任(xìnrèn)：动词，相信。
   Verb, to trust, to believe in.
2. 演(yǎn)：动词，通过技艺表现或再现。
   Verb, to perform, to play a role.
3. 表情(biǎoqíng)：名词，面部的不同情感表现。
   Noun, facial expression.
4. 活灵活现(huó líng huó xiàn)：成语，形容解释描写和亲眼见到的一样。
   Four-character idiom, lifelike, making people believe it is real.
5. 虚伪(xūwěi)：形容词，（指人的行为表现）不真实。
   Adjective, not honest, superficial, hypocritical.

píngshí bù shāo xiāng línshí bào fójiǎo

58. 平时 不烧 香，临时 抱 佛脚

No burning incenses when things are well, grasping at Buddha's feet when troubles come

◈ **Not prepared for trouble but ask for help only when problems occur**

谚语，贬义，强调临时准备，没有充分的时间做好准备。
Proverb, derogatory, emphasizing that a preparation is carried in a hurry, and it is not enough to avoid troubles.

Examples:

做事情不能平时不烧香，临时抱佛脚，而应该有备无患。

It is wrong to grab at Buddha's feet only when in troubles. One should always be prepared for contingencies.

A：明天就要考试了，看来今天要熬夜了。
B：你这是平时不烧香，临时抱佛脚。

A: We're going to have a test tomorrow. It looks like I'll have to pull another all-nighter.

B: If you had studied on a regular basis, this wouldn't be happening.

Tips

1. 烧香(shāo xiāng): 动词，一种敬拜神佛祖先的方式；烧，用火点燃；香，香料做成的细条。
   Verb, to burn incenses (in order to show respect toward gods, Buddha, or ancestors); shāo, to burn; xiāng, incense, a small stick made of aromatic materials.
2. 有备无患(yǒu bèi wú huàn)：成语，因为有了准备所以就不用担心了。
   Four-character idiom, to avoid problems by planning ahead.
3. 熬夜(áo yè)：动词，晚上晚睡或不睡觉。
   Verb, to stay up late or all night.

Q

qí lǘ kàn chàngběn zǒu zhe qiáo

59. 骑驴看 唱本——走 着 瞧

Reading a script while riding a donkey—let's wait and see what will happen next

◈ **A decision or result will come forth as a situation develops.**

歇后语，中性，表示有能力应付所有的情况，等待最后的结果。通常表示自己心中有数，对事情的结果有信心。

Two-part allegorical saying, neutral, denoting the certainty of knowing what will happen in the end; often used to indicate one has confidence in what will come out.

Examples:

今年的股市很难预测，究竟是熊市还是牛市，咱们骑驴看唱本——走着瞧吧。

It is difficult to predict whether this year's stock market will be a bear or a bull. Let's wait and see how things develop.

A：明天的比赛你准备也没有用，冠军一定是我。

B：是吗？咱们骑驴看唱本，走着瞧！

A: Your preparations won't make a difference on tomorrow's match. I'm definitely going to be the champion.

B: Really? Let's wait and see.

Tips

1. 股市(gǔshì)：名词，股票市场；股，股票；市，市场。
   Noun, stock market; (gǔ), as in (gǔpiào), stock; (shì), as in (shìchǎng), market.
2. 究竟(jiūjìng)：副词，用来加强语气，说话人非常想知道答案。
   Adverb, used to emphasize the urgent desire for answers.

60. 巧妇难为无米之炊

qiǎo fù nán wéi wú mǐ zhī chuī

Even a clever wife cannot cook a meal without rice.

◈ **People cannot do anything without necessary means or materials.**

谚语，中性，表示没有必要的条件就没办法达到要求。通常用来强调条件的重要性。

Proverb neutral, denoting that a result cannot be achieved without necessary resources; often used to emphasize the importance of supports.

Examples:

大学让我们组建一支一流的足球队，但是没有给我们任何拨款。巧妇难为无米之炊呀！

The university wanted us to build up a first class soccer team, but neglected to allocate any funds for it. Even a clever wife cannot make a meal without rice!

A：你完成我要的报告了吗？
B：一点资料都没有，你让我怎么写。巧妇难为无米之炊嘛！
A: Have you finished the report I wanted?
B: How can you expect me to do that without gathering data first? Even the best reporter can't write without material.

Tips

1. 一流(yīliú)：形容词，质量水平里的最高等级。
   Adjective, first class, the best kind.
2. 拨款(bō kuǎn)：动词，政府或上级分配资金。
   Verb, to allocate funds; noun, allocated fund.
3. 炊(chuī)：古代汉语，动词，做饭；名词，做饭这件事。
   Classical Chinese, verb, to cook a meal; noun, meal cooking.

qiāng dǎ chū tóu niǎo
61. 枪打出头鸟

The bird that sticks its head out gets shot.

People who stand out are more likely to be attacked.

◈ **A similar English expression: The nail that sticks up gets hammered down.**

谚语，中性，表示首先出现的就最容易受到打击。通常用来劝别人不要争先。

Proverb, neutral, denoting it is easy for the early emergence to attract attack; often used to persuade others not to stand out first.

Examples:

在总统选举时，枪打出头鸟，谁敢说提高税收，谁就会落选。

In the presidential election, any candidate who says anything about raising taxes is sticking his neck out and will be voted out.

A：大家都知道那个警察和黑帮有联系，可没人敢出来做证。

B：是啊，枪打出头鸟。他们担心会遭到报复。

A: Everybody knows that policeman is connected with the mafia, yet nobody dares to testify against him.

B: Yes, they are afraid of sticking their necks out for reprisals.

Tips

1. 谁……，谁就……(shéi (shuí)..., shéi (shuí) jiù...)：疑问代词表示任指，前一个谁表示任何人，后一个谁表示和前面一样的那个人。
   The first "shéi" refers to a type of person as an example, and the latter "shéi" points to someone who is similar to the example.
2. 黑帮(hēibāng)：名词，有组织的犯罪集团。
   Noun, mafia, gangs.
3. 遭到(zāodào)：动词，受到(伤害)。
   Verb, to get (hurt).

4. 报复(bàofù)：动词，被伤害者或其亲人朋友伤害那个伤害者。名词，被伤害者或其亲人朋友伤害伤害者的行为。
Verb, to retaliate to hurt the one who once hurt the others; noun, retaliation.

qiáng lóng yā bú guò dì tóu shé

62. 强龙压不过地头蛇

Even a powerful dragon cannot overwhelm a local snake.

◈ A strong power from the outside cannot defeat a local power.

谚语，中性，强调不熟悉当地环境就无法战胜当地的对手。
Proverb, neutral, denoting that it is hard to overcome local adversaries without knowing local situations.

Examples:

跨国公司常常主动找国内相关公司合作，毕竟强龙压不过地头蛇。与其竞争，不如合作。

Multinationals often choose to cooperate with domestic companies in China. When they cannot defeat local businesses, they prefer cooperation rather than competition.

A：要想消灭恐怖组织，先得除掉这个地方的军阀。

B：这可不是好办法。强龙压不过地头蛇呀。

A: To wipe out the terrorist cell in this area, we should first get rid of the local warlords.

B: I am not sure this is a good strategy since we cannot overcome local powers.

Tips

1. 毕竟(bìjìng)：副词，表示追根究底所得的结论；常用在肯定句中，强调原因或结果。
   Adverb, denoting that a conclusion is obtained through analysis; often used in affirmative sentences to emphasize a reason or result.
2. 与其……，不如……(yǔqí..., bùrú...)：表示选择关系的复句，前面的选择没有后面的选择好。
   Alternative clause, denoting the first choice is not as good as the second.
3. 军阀(jūnfá)：名词，有自己军队并控制一些区域的军人领导。
   Noun, warlord, a person who has both military and civil control over a region due to holding an armed force.

63. 青出于蓝而胜于蓝

qīng chū yú lán ér shèng yú lán

Indigo dye is bluer than the plant it comes from.

◈ **An apprentice is bound to surpass his master.**

成语，褒义，形容晚辈经过努力一定可以超越前辈。通常用来称赞晚辈。

Idiom, commendatory, denoting that younger generations can surpass the older generation if working hard; mostly used to praise the achievement of a younger generation.

Examples:

日本汽车制造业向美国学习了先进技术。现在，他们超过了美国。真是青出于[1]蓝而胜于[2]蓝。

The Japanese auto industry has learned advanced technologies from the States, and now they have surpassed the master. Indeed, the student has outperformed his teacher.

A：杰克的功夫越来越好了，现在都可以打败他师傅了。

B：很自然。青出于蓝但迟早要胜于蓝嘛。

A: Jack's Kung Fu is improving by leaps and bounds. He has progressed to the point where he can defeat his teacher.

B: It is only natural that the student will become better than the master sooner or later.

Tips

1. 于[1](yú[1])：介词，古汉语中为“从某处而来”的意思。
   Preposition, classical Chinese, meaning “from”.
2. 于[2](Yú[2])：用于比较，更加的意思。
   In the pattern of “A + adjective + Yu + B”, denoting comparison, meaning “more than”.
3. 越来越…(yuèláiyuè…)：表示程度变化。
   Adverb, more and more, denoting the change of degrees.

qíngrén yǎn lǐ chū xīshī
64. 情人 眼 里出 西施

A girl becomes Xi Shi in the eyes of her lover.

◈ **A similar English expression: Beauty lies in the eyes of the beholder.**

谚语，中性，表示因为喜爱而过高评价自己所爱的人或事物。通常用来指评价是出于感觉因素，所以缺乏理性。

Proverb, neutral, denoting that someone or something is over-praised due to personal preferences; mostly used to point out an evaluation that is not objective or well-grounded.

Examples:

我觉得我家乡的月亮比别的地方的更亮。这也算是情人眼里出西施吧！

I feel that the moon in my hometown is brighter than that in all other places. Isn't it because beauty is in the eyes of the beholder?

A：他怎么鼓励女朋友参加选美呢？我觉得不可能有任何希望。

B：你不知道情人眼里出西施吗？

A: How could he encourage his girlfriend to compete in the beauty contest? She doesn't stand a chance in my opinion.

B: Don't you know love is bind indeed?

Tips

1. 西施(Xīshī)：人名，一位中国古代有名的美女。
   Person's name, a well-known ancient Chinese beauty.
2. 鼓励(gǔlì)：动词，支持，激励。
   Verb, to encourage, to inspire.
3. 任何(rènhé)：代词，无论什么，随便什么。
   Pronoun, whatever, any.

qiū hòu de màzha bèngda bù liǎo jǐ tiān le

65. 秋后的蚂蚱——蹦跶不了几天了

A grasshopper after autumn—its days are numbered

◈ **To be short lived**

歇后语，贬义，表示坏人或不符合要求的事物不会长久。通常用来告诫坏人不要继续一错再错，或者指出不符合要求的事物必然会被淘汰。

Two-part allegorical saying, derogatory, denoting evil people or things cannot last long; often used to predict that someone or something has its doomed fate.

Examples:

油耗大的汽车是秋后的蚂蚱——蹦跶不了几天了。

Gas guzzling cars are bound to be short lived, just like the grasshoppers after the autumn.

A：这位离任州长又任命了几个亲信，想阻止改革。
B：别急，他是秋后的蚂蚱——蹦跶不了几天了。

A: This lame duck governor has appointed his cronies so as to block reforms.

B: Don't worry about it. His days are numbered.

Tips

1. 蹦跶(bèngda)：动词，在一个范围内来回跳，用来指痛苦地坚持。

   Verb, to jump around, often used to imply "to struggle painfully".

2. 亲信(qīnxìn)：名词，身边值得信赖的人。

   Noun, trusted follower.

R

rè guō shàng de mǎyǐ

66. 热锅 上 的蚂蚁

Ants crawling in a hot pan

◈ **People in deep trouble and anxious to find way out**

谚语，中性，形容非常着急。

Proverb, neutral, describing the degree of severe anxiety.

Examples:

她的儿子已经两天没有回家了，一点儿消息也没有。她急得像热锅上的蚂蚁一样。

Her son has been missing for two days, and there's been no news of him since. Like an ant in a hot pan, the poor mother is stricken with grief and anxiety.

A：你怎么着急得像热锅上的蚂蚁一样？发生什么事儿了？

B：还有十分钟婚礼就开始了。可是新郎还没有到。真急死人。

A: How come you are fidgeting about so much? What's going on?

B: The wedding is going to start in ten minutes and the groom still isn't here. It is nerve wracking.

Tips

1. 还有……就开始了(háiyǒu...jiù kāishǐ le)：表示马上，离事情发生的时间很短。
Denoting that an event will happen soon.
2. 新郎(xīnláng)：名词，结婚时的男方。
Noun, bridegroom, a man who is about to get married or has just been married.

67. 肉包子打狗——有去无回
ròu bāozi dǎgǒu yǒu qù wú huí

A meat ball thrown at a dog—a total loss

◈ **Something is given or lost to those who do not reciprocate or show gratitude**

歇后语，贬义，表示提供的东西没有任何回复，一去不复返，或者给予的帮助得不到回报。

Two-part allegorical saying, derogatory, denoting that things provided to others cannot get any reply and are gone forever, or that help to others cannot bring in any reciprocal treatment.

Examples:

如果这个地区社会混乱，任何投资都是肉包子打狗——有去无回。

If there is no order in this country, any investment will be a waste of money.

A：他从我这里借了很多书，但从来不还。我这不是肉包子打狗—有去无回吗？

B：你的看法有点偏激。也许他忘了。你提醒他一下吧。

A: He borrowed many books from me but never brought them back. To me, my books are just like meat balls being thrown to a dog, without any hope for return.

B: I think you're being biased. Maybe he forgot. You can just remind him of it. You cannot expect to improve people's appreciation of art overnight.

Tips

1. 社会混乱(shèhuì hùnluàn)：名词短语，社会进入没有秩序的状态。
   Noun phrase, social chaos.
2. 从来(cónglái)：副词，从开始到现在。
   Adverb, meaning "from beginning to now".
3. 偏激(piānjī)：形容词，思想言论等偏向一方，不公平。
   Adjective, extreme, radical, often used to describe one's views or words.
4. 提醒(tíxǐng)：动词，引起注意，帮助想起。
   Verb, to remind, to call attention to.

S

sān gè chòu píjiàng dǐng ge Zhūgě Liàng

68. 三个臭皮匠，顶个诸葛亮

Three tanners together are equal to one Zhūgě Liàng.

The intelligence of three people equals that of a single smart person.

◈ A similar English expression: Two heads are better than one.

谚语，褒义，强调集体智慧的重要性。

Proverb, commendatory, emphasizing the important of collective wisdom.

Examples:

我们负责运动会开幕式的安全。三个臭皮匠，顶个诸葛亮，大家一起制定一个方案。

We are put in charge of security at the sports games' opening ceremony. More heads are better than one, so let's make a security plan as a team.

A：如今的科学研究离不开集体智慧。三个臭皮匠，顶个诸葛亮。

B：是吗？我觉得一个诸葛亮能顶一百个臭皮匠。哪个著名的科学里程碑不是个人创立的？

A: Scientific research depends on the collective wisdom. Many heads are better than one.

B: Are you sure? I think the other way round. Sometimes one wise man is worth a hundred mediocres. Most great scientific inventions are done by individuals, isn't it?

Tips

1. 负责(fùzé)：动词，承担责任。
   Verb, to be in charge of, to be responsible for.
2. 开幕式(kāimùshì)：重大事件正式开始的仪式。
   Noun, opening ceremony.
3. 顶(dǐng)：动词，相当，等于。
   Verb, to be equivalent to, equal to.
4. 诸葛亮(Zhūgě Liàng)：人名，古代中国有名的政治家和军事家。他因为聪明和善于谋虑而著名。
   Person's name, an ancient Chinese politician and military strategist, well-known for his great wisdom and resourcefulness.
5. 离不开(líbukāi)：动补短语，表示不能分开。
   Verb-compliment phrase, cannot do without.
6. 哪个A不是B(nǎge A, bú shì B)：表示反问，每个A都是B。
   Rhetorical question, denoting every A is B.

sān xīn èr yì

69. 三心二意

Three minds, two thoughts

◈ **Not concentrated, absent-minded, or undecided**

成语，贬义，形容非常不专心。

Four-character idiom, derogatory, meaning "not committed", "not concentrated", or "not whole-hearted".

Examples:

你学开车时，不可三心二意，否则会出事的。

You have to concentrate when learning how to drive. Otherwise, accidents will happen.

A：北大和清华都给我寄录取通知书了。你说去哪个学校比较好？

B：不要三心二意了。还是北大吧。

A: I have been accepted by both Beida and Qinghua. In your opinion, which one is better for me?

B: Don't be indecisive. Personally, I think that you'd be better off at Beida.

Tips

1. 北大(Běidà)：专有名词，北京大学的简称。
   proper noun, short term for Peking University in Chinese.
2. 清华(Qīnghuá)：专有名词，清华大学的简称。
   proper noun, short term for Tsinghua University in Chinese.
3. 还是……吧(háishì...ba)：表示建议。
   Denoting a suggestion.

70. 杀鸡给猴看

shā jī gěi hóu kàn

Killing a chicken to warn the monkey

◈ **To warn somebody by punishing someone else**

谚语，中性，表示用惩罚个别人或犯小错者来警告多数人或有大错者。通常用来强调个别惩罚的全局意义。

Proverb, neutral, denoting that a warning is given to a whole group through punishing one of them, or by punishing people with trivial mistakes to prevent any further blunder; often used to emphasize the overall impact of punishing an individual.

Examples:

员工迟到的问题最近非常普遍。所以，项目主任今天当众批评了小王，就是杀鸡给猴看啊。

Tardiness has been a widespread problem at our workplace. Then, the program director decided to make an example of Wang today by publicly reprimanding him for coming in late.

A：昨天学校处理了两个酗酒的学生。

B：那是杀鸡给猴看。咱们学校毕竟是个禁酒的校园呀。

A: Yesterday, two students who were caught drinking were disciplined by the university.

B: This is a typical case of making an example out of someone. After all, we are a dry campus.

Tips

1. 普遍(pǔbiàn)：形容词，指现象、特点、情况等的广泛。
   Adjective, common, widespread.
2. 当众(dāngzhòng)：副词，面对着很多人；当，面对着；众，很多人。
   Adverb, in front of many people, in public, publically; dāng, in the face of; zhòng, many people.
3. 酗酒(xù jiǔ)：动词，特别爱喝酒并且常常喝醉。
   Verb, to drink excessively.

shān wài yǒu shān rénwài yǒu rén

71. 山外有山，人外有人

There are mountains beyond mountains and more capable people besides those we know.

◈ **There is always something or somebody better out there.**

谚语，中性，表示强者之外还有强者，好的东西之外也会有更好的。通常用来建议别人要谦虚，或者表达对某人或某事物的高度认可。

Two-part allegorical saying, neutral, denoting that there are strong and capable people besides what we know and there are better things out there; often used to advise others to be modest or to show recognition to better things.

Examples:

没想到这个前世界冠军居然输给了一个无名小卒！还是山外有山，人外有人啊！

What a surprise! The unknown opponent actually defeated the former world champion. It is true that there are more talents than we have known.

A：你画得太好了。不会有人超过你的。

B：哪里哪里。山外有山，人外有人。比我厉害的人多的是。

A: You are so good at painting that nobody can surpass you on it.

B: Not really but thanks. I know, there are many people who are actually better.

Tips

1. 居然(jūrán)：副词，没有想到。
   Adverb, unexpectedly, to one's surprise.
2. 无名小卒(wú míng xiǎo zú)：成语，非常平常的人；无名，没有名字；小卒，小兵。
   Four-character idiom; nobody, a person with no significance; wúmíng, without a name; xiǎozú, an insignificant soldier.
3. 超过(chāoguò)：动词，从后边赶上，比…更多。
   Verb, to surpass, to overtake, to exceed.
4. 哪里哪里(Nǎli nǎli)：口语，在回答别人称赞时用于表示谦虚，意思是您过奖了。

Colloquial, literally meaning "where where", generally used to respond to compliments and to demonstrate humbleness, meaning "not really" or "you are too generous in giving me the compliments."

shān zhōng wú lǎohǔ hóuzi chēng dàiwang
72. 山中无老虎,猴子称大王

When tigers are not in the mountain, monkeys are king.

An average person may become the leader in the absence of superior people

◈ **A similar English expression: Among the blind the one-eyed man is king.**

谚语,中性,表示因为更高水平的人不在,所以次等级的人有了优势。

Proverb, neutral, denoting that when the most capable people or objects are absent, the lesser ones will stand out.

Examples:

马教授被大家选为院长,但他告诉大家,"我是山中无老虎,猴子称大王。"

After Professor Ma was elected president of the college, he modestly told everybody that, "I am only holding the position in the absence of someone more talented".

A：祝贺呀！你的发明获得了全国科技一等奖。

B：那是山中无老虎，猴子称大王了！高手们今年没有参赛。

A: Congrats! Your invention won the first prize at the National Science and Technology Competition.

B: I won only because the most talented people were absent from this year's competition.

Tips

1. 被……为(bèi... wéi)：在句型"A+被+B+verb+为+C"中，表示因为B，所以A成了C。

   In the pattern "A + bèi + B + verb + wéi + C", denoting A turns into C as a result of B.

2. 大王(dàiwang)：名词，山寨头目，某一地区内的首领。

   Noun, head of a gang in a mountain, a leader or chief in a region.

3. 科技(kējìè)：名词，科学和技术。

   Noun, science and technology.

4. 高手(gāoshǒu)：名词，水平很高的人。

   Noun, proficient, expert.

shòusǐ de luòtuo bǐ mǎ dà

73. 瘦死 的骆驼 比马大

A camel starved to death is still bigger than a horse.

◈ **Wealthy people or prosperous organizations are still more powerful than others even when they are in trouble.**

谚语，中性，强调即使一流人才或者机构不是最好的状态，但是依然比其他竞争者强很多。通常用来告诫他人别小看了处于弱势的强者。

Proverb, neutral, emphasizing that the first rank talents or organizations still have strong competitive power even in their times of difficulties; often used to advise people not to underestimate the strong in their downturn.

Examples:

虽然这家大公司将要申请破产，但瘦死的骆驼比马大，其他公司很难代替它的老大地位。

Although this big company is going to file for bankruptcy, it is still more influential than most others. So far nobody is able to replace its number one position yet.

A：为什么那位总裁退休后还那么有影响力？
B：人家毕竟当过总裁。瘦死的骆驼比马大呀。
A: Why is that retired CEO still so influential?
B: After all, he was in a position of power. Though retired, he is still what he is made of.

Tips

1. 骆驼(luòtuo)：名词，一种生活在沙漠中的动物。
   Noun, camel, an animal living in the desert with one hump or two.
2. 比(bǐ)：在句型“A比B+形容词”，表示A的程度更高。
   In the pattern “A+bǐ+B+adjective”, denoting that A and B have the same property or characteristic but A is more so.

3. 老大(lǎodà)：名词，具有绝对权力的个人、组织。
Noun, the big one, referring to people or organizations with some absolute advantages or superiorities.
4. 总裁(zǒngcái)：名词，公司的最高管理人员。
Noun, president, CEO, or chairman of a company.

shù dà zhāo fēng
74. 树大招风

Big trees catch much wind.

◈ **Wealth and fame bring public attention and jealousy.**

成语，中性，形容出名的人或机构会受到过多的关注。通常用来说明名人或者著名机构因一个失误就会有太多的社会压力。

Four-character idiom, neutral, denoting that famous people or institutions get more attentions from the public; mostly used to denote that famous people or institutions are under more social pressures due to the public attention.

Examples:

人越出名，越要低调行事，小心树大招风啊！

The more famous you get, the more careful you have to be, since you will always be in the public eye.

A：作为著名的电视主持人，即使一个小小的口误也会惹来公众的一片指责。

B：没办法，树大招风嘛！

A: As a well known TV anchor, he will bring criticism upon himself for the slightest mishap.

B: What can you do? Public figures attract more attention.

Tips

1. 越……越……(yuè...yuè...)：表示程度随着条件的变化而变化。
   The more...the more...; denoting the changes contingent on the changing environment.
2. 低调(dīdiào)：形容词，谦虚谨慎，不急于显示自己的能力。
   Adjective, low key; low profile; here used as an adverb, meaning "in a low profile manner."
3. 即使……也……(jíshǐ...yě...)："即使"的后面是一个假设，说话人不会改变的看法或认定的结果。
   "jíshǐ (even though)" is followed by a hypothesis, and "yě" is always followed by a statement or view as believed by the speaker.

shuǐ huǒ bù róng

75. 水火不容

Water and fire cannot be harmonized.

Incompatible or irreconcilable

◈ A similar English expression: Oil and water do not mix.

成语，中性，表示两者相互对立，不能共处同一环境。通常用来说明矛盾不可能解决。

Four-character idiom, neutral, denoting that the two sides cannot or get along or intermingle; mostly used to indicate that contradiction cannot be reconciled.

Examples:

张女士不愧是婚姻问题的专家。她经常能让水火不容的两口子找到和解的机会。

Ms. Zhang is indeed an expert on marriage. Through her counseling, incompatible couples may have a good chance at reconciliation.

A：这两个家族相互仇视，甚至水火不容。

B：我听说那是因为几代人以前的矛盾。现在他们的年轻人早该不计前嫌，言归于好。

A: The two families are hostile to each other, even to the degree of not being able to co-exist.

B: I heard that it comes from their family conflicts a couple of generations ago. By now those young people should have given up the previous hatred and been reconciled.

Tips

1. 不愧(búkuì)：副词，常用格式是"A+不愧是/为+B"，A值得有B这样的称号或头衔。
Adverb, in the pattern of "A + búkuìshì/wéi + B", meaning that A is B.

2. 两口子(liǎngkǒuzi):名词短语,口语词,夫妻。
Noun, colloquial, a couple.
3. 仇视(chóushì):动词,对别人不友好,把别人当做仇人看待。
Verb, to be hostile to, to regard as an enemy.
4. 几代人(jǐdàirén):名词短语,不同年龄段和辈分的人。
Noun phrase, a couple of generations, or people of different ages.
5. 计(jì):动词,计较,考虑。
Verb, to think over, to consider.
6. 前嫌(qiánxián):名词,过去的仇恨和不满。
Noun, previous hatred and grudge.
7. 言归于好(yánguīyúhǎo):成语,重新和好。
Idiom, to be reconciled.

shuǐ zhōng yuè, jìng zhōng huā
76. 水 中 月,镜 中 花

The moon in water, a flower in a mirror

◈ **Things that are not real, things that cannot come ture or only exit in illusion**

成语,也作"水月镜花",中性,指不实际的事物,尤其是虚幻的景象。
idiom, neutral, referring to things that are not real or practical, especially those illusory images or ideas.

Examples:

如果不努力，所有的梦想都是水中月，镜中花。

If we don't work hard, our dreams can only stay in our heads but never come true.

A：我不可以追求完美的爱情吗？

B：最好别这样。所谓完美的爱情大多是水中月镜中花。

A: Why cannot I pursue a perfect relationship?

B: You better not. The so-called perfect relationship is mostly unreal.

Tips

1. 完美(wánměi)：形容词，非常好的，没有缺点的。
   Adjective, very good, flawless.
2. 所谓(suǒwèi)：大家所说的，大家所认为的。
   What is called, so-called, or what people think or call.

sǐ mǎ dāng zuò huó mǎ yī

77. 死马当 做活马医

To treat a dead horse as if it is still alive

◈ **To try without much hope for success**

谚语，中性，表示已经知道无法弥补，但是还是要想办法处理。通常用来强调对现实情况的无奈，但是又不能放弃。

Proverb, neutral, denoting that people continue to strive even with little or no chance to succeed; often used to emphasize the hopelessness of actual situation but still people won't give up.

Examples:

这支足球队是一支没有任何希望的队伍，但新上任的教练发誓要死马当做活马医，三年扭转局面。

The football team is hopeless, but the new coach vows to try his very best and turn it around in three years.

A：这车都撞成这样了，还能修好吗？
B：不太清楚，修修试试吧。死马当做活马医。
A: This car's badly damaged. Do you think it can still be fixed?
B: I don't know, but I might as well give it a shot.

Tips

1. 发誓(fāshì)：动词，说出表示决心的话。
   Verb, to swear, to pledge.
2. 扭转(niǔzhuǎn)：动词，使事物的发展方向由不利到有利。
   Verb, to turn around, to reverse the tide (for a better situation).
3. 撞(zhuàng)：动词，碰在了一起，例如，撞墙，撞车，撞见。
   Verb, to hit on, to crash into, such as in zhuàngqiáng (to hit a wall), zhuàngchē (to bump into another car), and zhuàngjiàn (to run into someone).

sǐ zhū bú pà kāi shuǐ tàng

78. 死猪不怕开水烫

A dead pig is not afraid of boiling water.

◈ **People in serious distress don't care if the situation becomes worse.**

谚语，贬义，表示无所顾忌，按照自己的选择做事，完全不担心坏的后果。通常用来指出顽固的人不改变自己的做事方法，或拒绝与人合作。

Proverb, derogatory,describing people to behave totally according to their own wills without consideration of any possible bad consequence; often used to criticize people to be stubborn or refuse to cooperate with the others.

Examples:

被俘的极端分子都是死猪不怕开水烫，拒绝回答任何问题。

The captured extremists are fearless since things cannot get any worse for them, and have refused to answer any questions.

A: 老张被撤职以后，他对公司的新政策更加反对，还在网络上发表文章揭露公司的内幕。

B: 他这是死猪不怕开水烫，反正也没有什么可担心失去的了。

A: We'll have an exam tomorrow. How come you haven't started reviewing?

B: I'm going to fail anyway. Why bother? It can't get any worse.

Tips

1. 被俘(bèi fú)：动词词组，被抓住，成为俘虏。
   Verb phrase, to be captured.
2. 烫(tàng)：动词，因温度太高而疼痛。
   Verb, to scald, to get hurt due to touching something very hot.
3. 拒绝(jùjué)：动词，明确地表示不答应。
   Verb, to reject, to refuse.
4. 撤职(chè zhí)：动词，撤销职务，取消职责。
   Verb, to dismiss from a position, to remove from an office.
5. 网络(wǎngluò)：名词，互联网。
   Noun, internet.
6. 内幕(nèimù)：名词，内部的信息，常指不好的事情。
   Noun, inside information or stories, especially the negative ones.
7. 什么(shénme)：疑问代词任指，表示所有的东西或无论什么东西，可用在“也”、“都”前或“不论”、“无论”、“不管”后。
   Question pronoun, referring to all things or everything, often used before “yě”, “dōu”, or after “wúlùn”, “bùguǎn”, etc.

T

tí xīn diào dǎn

79. 提心吊胆

With heart suspended and gall bladder hung

◈ **To be very anxious and cautious**

成语，中性，形容非常担心。

Four-character idiom, neutral, denoting that someone is worried and on edge.

Examples:

他是新来的吊车司机，经验很少，工作时总是提心吊胆，怕出安全问题。

As a crane operator without much experience, he is always anxious and worried about possible safety problems.

A：怎么[1]每次坐飞机你都提心吊胆的呢？

B：说实话，我有严重的恐高症。怎么[2]也克服不了。

A: Why do you get so anxious whenever you are flying in an airplane?

B: To be honest with you, I have a serious acrophobia. I just cannot get over it no matter how hard I try.

Tips

1. 吊车(diàochē)：名词，抬起重物的一种机器。
   Noun, crane, hoist.
2. 怎么[1](zěnme)：疑问代词，表示“为什么”的意思。
   Question pronoun, meaning “why”.
3. 恐高症(kǒnggāozhèng)：名词，站在高处感到恐惧的病；恐，恐惧；高，高度；症，病，病状，例如忧郁症、绝症、顽症。
   Noun, acrophobia, an abnormal fear of high places; kǒng, as in kǒngjù, fear; gāo, as in gāodù, height; zhèng, disease, symptom, such as yōuyùzhèng (depression), juézhèng (incurable disease), and wánzhèng (disease that is hard to be cured).
4. 怎么[2](zěnme)：疑问代词任指，表示所有的办法或无论用什么办法，可用在“也”、“都”前或“不论”、“无论”、“不管”后。
   Question pronoun, referring to all things in general and here, denoting whatever methods or ways; often used before “yě”, “dōu”, or after “búlùn”, “wúlùn”, “bùguǎn”, etc.

tiānxià wūyā yìbān hēi

80. 天下 乌鸦一般 黑

All ravens under heaven are equally black.

◈ **Evil people or organizations are the same everywhere.**

谚语，贬义，表示坏的现象到处都是。通常用来表达对普遍存在的坏现象的强烈不满。

Proverb, derogatory, denoting there are bad people or things everywhere; often used to show strong discontent to bad people in all places.

Examples:

我的房东最近也突然要涨很多房租。这也算是天下乌鸦一般黑吧。

My landlord also suddenly wanted to raise my rent by a large amount. Is it true that greedy people are the same everywhere?

A：我本想这个国际大公司会公平地对待员工，现在意识到我错了。

B：天下乌鸦一般黑，到哪儿都一样。

A: I thought this multinational company would treat employees fairly, but now I realize I was wrong.

B: There are bad bosses everywhere.

Tips

1. 一般(yìbān)：副词，一样，同样。
   Adverb, the same as.
2. 意识到(yìshi dào)：动词短语
   Verbal phrase, to be aware of, to realize.
3. 哪儿(nǎr)：疑问代词任指，表示所有的地方，可用在"也"、"都"前或"不论"、"无论"、"不管"后。
   Question pronoun, refering to all places in general, meaning everywhere or all places; often be used before "yě", "dōu" or after "búlùn", "wúlùn", "bùguǎn", etc.

tiě gōngjī　　yì máo bù bá

81. 铁公鸡——一毛 不拔

An iron rooster—not giving off a feather

◈ **A very stingy person**

歇后语，贬义，形容非常吝啬。

Two-part allegorical saying, derogatory, describing stingy people

Examples:

王先生是个著名的慈善家。可是对懒惰的亲戚，他就是只铁公鸡——一毛不拔。

Mr. Wang is a famed philanthropist, but he is very stingy when it comes to spending money on his lazy relatives.

A：地震后，大家都纷纷捐款，但是咱们公司没捐一分钱。

B：你不知道我们的老板是出了名的铁公鸡吗？

A: After the earthquake, everybody made donations. But our company did not give one cent!

B: Haven't you heard that our boss is an "iron rooster"?

Tips

1. 慈善家(císhànjiā)：名词，经常从事慈善活动的人士；家，掌握特殊技能从事某种专业的人，例如作家、科学家、艺术家、画家等。

Noun, philanthropist, a person who always contributes to charitable work; jiā, a professional with special knowledge and skills, such as zuòjiā (writer), kēxuéjiā (scientist), yìshùjiā (artist), huàjiā (painter), etc.

2. 懒惰(lǎnduò)：形容词，不喜欢费体力或脑力。
   Adjective, lazy, indolent.
3. 拔(bá)：动词，用力拉出来。
   Verb, to pull.

82. 兔子不吃窝边草 (tùzi bù chī wō biān cǎo)

A rabbit won't eat grass near its rabbit hole.

No one commit any unsavory acts in his own neighborhood.

◈ A similar English expression: The fox preys farthest from home.

谚语，中性，通常用来说明坏人不会伤害和自己亲近的人。
Proverb, neutral, often used to indicate that bad people or organizations won't infringe upon the benefit of people in their close proximity.

Examples:

俗话说兔子不吃窝边草，但现在很多人专门赚朋友的钱。

It is said the fox preys farthest from home, yet many people make money out of their friends.

A：邻居们都觉得他是个好人。很难相信他是个抢劫犯。

B：兔子不吃窝边草嘛！

A: All neighbors thought he was a good man and couldn't believe that he was a robber.

B: He does not prey in his neighborhood.

Tips

1. 窝(wō)：名词，动物的巢穴。
   Noun, nest or hole, animal's resting place.
2. 专门(zhuānmén)：副词，专一从事某事或研究某门学问。
   Adverb, in the pattern "zhuānmén + verb", meaning "to be specialized in".
3. 抢劫犯(qiǎngjiéfàn)：名词，以暴力获得财物的罪犯；犯，罪犯，例如杀人犯、强奸犯、政治犯。
   Noun, robber; fàn, criminal, convicted person, such as in shārénfàn (murder), qiángjiānfàn (rapist), and zhèngzhìfàn (political prisoner).

W

wáng pó mài guā—— zì mài zì kuā

83. 王婆卖瓜——自卖自夸

Old lady Wang comes to sell melons —praising all along what she sells.

◈ **One overpraises one's own goods.**

A similar English expression: Every potter praises his own pot.

歇后语，中性，或贬义，过多夸赞自已的东西，甚至自我吹嘘。

Two-part allegorical saying, neutral, or derogatory, indicating that people praise too much of their own things, even indulge in self-glorification.

Examples:

不是王婆卖瓜——自卖自夸。我们的产品是真的很好。

It is not like old lady Wang overpraising her own goods. Indeed, our products are truely excellent.

A：你怎么看王婆卖瓜—自卖自夸这样的行为？
B：这也算是一种推销的方法吧，虽说不见得很高明。

A: What do you think when seeing people blowing trumpet for their merchandise?

B: Well, it's a way for sales promotion, even though it might not be a very brilliant method.

Tips

1. 夸(kuā)：动词，称赞，讲大话。

   Verb, to praise, to boast, to exaggerate.

2. 不见得(bújiàndé)：短语，不一定。

   A phrase, not necessarily, might not be.

3. 高明(gāomíng)：形容词，(见解)独特，(技艺)高超。

   Adjective, unique (in opinion), superb (in skills).

X

xiā māo pèng zháo sǐ hàozi

84. 瞎猫碰着死耗子

A blind cat happens to catch a dead mouse.

Good things happen by pure luck.

◈ **A similar English expression: A blind man may catch the hare.**

歇后语，贬义，强调好的结果不是因为有好的能力，只是因为有好运气。

Two-part allegorical saying, derogatory, emphasizing the good results are obtained by luck or chance.

Examples:

他第一次买彩票就中了大奖。真是瞎猫碰着了死耗子呀。

He wins the lottery the first time buying it. This is a pure luck, like a blind cat catching a dead mouse.

A：你在股市里赚了不少钱呀。教我几招怎么样？

B：别开玩笑了！都是瞎猫碰着了死耗子。

A: You have made so much money in stocks! How about show me a few tricks?

B: Don't kid me. All my trades were actually pure luck.

Tips

1. 彩票(cǎipiào)：名词，印有数字的抽彩用的奖券。
   Noun, lottery ticket.
2. 招(zhāo)：名词，口语，手法、窍门、招数。
   Noun, colloquial, skill, trick, and method.

85. 小葱拌豆腐——一清二白

xiǎo cōng bàn dòufu —— yì qīng èr bái

Green onion mixes with tofu—one is green and another is white.

◈ **Things are clearly distinguishable from each other with a clear cut.**

歇后语，中性，强调非常清楚，没有任何可怀疑的。

Two-part allegorical saying, neutral, emphasizing clarity of situations.

Examples:

你现在是公司的会计了。记账要小葱拌豆腐——一清二白。

You are company's accountant now. You should keep a clear and straight record.

A：电视台将那个节目的主持人赶走了。听说新来的主持人搞了点儿鬼。

B：这是小葱拌豆腐——一清二白。别人不走，他怎么进来？

A: The TV station forced out the current host from the show. I heard the new host had a hand in this.

B: Obviously so. How else could that new person get into the show?

Tips

1. 会计(kuàijì)：名词，管理财务工作，管理财务工作的人。
   Noun, accounting, accountant.
2. 拌(bàn)：动词，把不同的东西混合在一起。
   Verb, to stir and mix.
3. 搞鬼(gǎo guǐ)：动词，暗中使用不正当的计谋。
   Verb, to do things behind another's back.

xiào lǐ cáng dāo

86. 笑里 藏 刀

To hide a knife behind smiles

Sinister intentions are masked under the disguise of goodwills.

◈ A similar English expression: The bait hides the hook.

成语，贬义，形容表面友善，但实际内心阴险。通常用来告诫他人别被表面的友善迷惑。

Four-character idiom, derogatory, describing people being seemingly nice but sinister inside; often used to warn others not to be deluded by superficial kindness.

Examples:

他学会了笑里藏刀，不露真相。

He has learned to hide his true intentions behind pleasant smiles and not to reveal his true colors.

A：新来的经理对大家非常友好。

B：他可能是笑里藏刀。我听说他裁员的时候是毫不留情的。

A: That new manager is very friendly to everybody.

B: It might be just a cover. I heard he showed no mercy when it comes to laying off people.

Tips

1. 藏(cáng)：动词，收存起来。
   Verb, to hide; to cover.
2. 露(lòu)：动词，展现出来。
   Verb, to expose; to disclose.
3. 裁员(cáiyuán)：动词，解雇员工。
   Verb, to lay off people.
4. 毫不留情(háo bù liú qíng)：成语，没有一点同情心。
   Four-character idiom, to show no mercy.

xīn jí chī bù liǎo rè dòufu

87. 心急 吃不了 热豆腐

One cannot eat hot tofu in a hurry.

Impatience will not solve problems.

◈ **A similar English expression: Haste makes waste.**

谚语，中性，表示如果着急就做不好任何事情。通常用来劝他人要有耐心。

Proverb, neutral, denoting that things cannot be done well in a hurry; often used to persuade others to be patient.

Examples:

学好一门外语需要很长的时间，心急吃不了热豆腐。

It takes a long time to master a foreign language. Rome, after all, was not built in a day.

A：我们急需一位中英文都优秀的大学生。你们找到这样的人了吗？

B：要知道心急吃不了热豆腐呀。耐心多等几天，肯定能找到。

A: We desperately need a college student who can speak both Chinese and English fluently. Have you found one for us yet?

B: You know rushing the selection process certainly will not guarantee the best result. Wait with patience for a couple of more days. We will get it done for sure.

Tips

1. 优秀(yōuxiù)：形容词，非常好。
   Adjective, excellent, outstanding.
2. 耐心(nàixīn)：形容词，不着急，心情不烦躁。
   Adjective, patient.

xuě shàng jiā shuāng

88. 雪 上 加 霜

To add frost on top of snow

◈ **To make things worse**

成语，贬义，表示祸事接二连三，情况继续恶化。

Four-character idiom, derogatory, denoting that disasters or mishaps come one after another, and a situation is worsened.

Examples:

他们的航班晚点了，很晚才到酒店，然后又发现雪上加霜的事情——酒店已经取消了他们的预定。

Their flight was delayed and thus they reached to the hotel quite late. Unfortunately things getting worse, they found out the hotel had cancelled their room reservation.

A：这个运动员的丑闻对我们公司的形象不利。我们应该取消他代言人的地位。

B：人家现在正是困难时期，咱们就不要雪上加霜了。

A: That athlete's scandal is not good for our company's image. We should withdraw our endorsement.

B: He is in trouble and we should probably avoid making things worse for him.

Tips

1. 晚点(wǎndiǎn)：比预计的时间晚。
   Adjective, late, delayed, behind schedule.
2. 对……不利(duì...búlì)：对……有害或没有好处。
   Not good for, causing harm to.

Y

yǎba chī huánglián　yǒu kǔ shuōbùchū

89. 哑巴吃 黄连——有 苦 说 不出

A mute person eats coptis—unable to tell others how bitter it is.

◈ **People are unable to communicate their sufferings or losses.**

歇后语，中性，表示受了委屈或损失只能忍受。

Two-part allegorical saying, neutral, denoting that people who have no way to complain have to endure the loss and unfairness silently.

Examples:

最近他在期货里损失了几百万。哑巴吃黄连——有苦说不出呀。

Recently, he lost several million dollars in futures. Yet he has no venue to tell his losses.

A: 今天明明是那个客户不对，你怎么不反驳他啊？

B: 客户是上帝，我们也是哑巴吃黄连——有苦说不出啊。

A: It was definitely the customer who was at fault. Why didn't you talk back?

B: The customer is always right in this business. We have to keep our complaints to ourselves.

Tips

1. 期货(qīhuò)：名词，按时在未来市场交易的股票或其他商品。

   Noun, futures, the commodities or stocks to be exchanged in the future.

2. 黄连(huánglián)：名词，一种可以做中药的味苦的植物。

   Noun, coptis; can be used as Chinese medicine, with a very bitter taste.

3. 反驳(fǎnbó)：动词，提出反对的理由否定别人的看法。

   Verb, to refute.

yī ge bāzhǎng pāi bù xiǎng

90. 一个巴掌 拍不响

One palm cannot make a sound.

◈ **A similar English expression: It takes two to make a quarrel. One person or one side cannot start trouble by themselves.**

gū zhǎng nán míng

孤掌 难鸣

One cannot accomplish much without help.

◈ **A similar English expression: You can´t catch a chicken with one hand.**

一个巴掌拍不响表示矛盾是由双方造成的，通常用来建议当事者从对方的角度考虑问题。孤掌难鸣表示势单力薄，靠一方的力量不能成事。

Denoting that both sides play a role for things to happen; often used to suggest both sides should take responsibility. Though essentially the two expressions mean the same connotatively, they have opposite denotations. The former is often used to urge all parties involved in disputes or conflicts to reflect on their own responsibilities or wrong-doings; the latter points out the importance of cooperation.

Examples:

他们两个家族之间的矛盾冲突已经有几十年了。我看一个巴掌拍不响，双方都有责任。

The conflicts between the two families have been going on for decades. I think both sides bear some responsibility, since it takes two sides to have a fight.

A：老王，我觉得咱们公司的管理体制有点儿落后，现在市场竞争这么激烈，必须及时改进啊！

B：我同意你的看法，可是老板们都认为应该维持现状，我也是孤掌难鸣啊。

A: Lao Wang, in my view, our company's management is quite outdated. In a market with such fierce competitions like we have now, we have to catch up fast!

B: I am with you. But most our managers want to maintain status. I cannot make any move alone.

Tips

1. 冲突(chōngtū)：名词，对立和不相容的情况。
   Noun, conflict, dispute.
2. 巴掌(bāzhǎng)：名词，连接手腕和手指的部位。
   Noun, palm.
3. 孤(gū)：形容词，古代汉语，一个，单独。
   Adjective, classical Chinese, single, alone.

yì rén dé dào jī quǎn shēng tiān
91. 一人得道，鸡犬升天

Once a man achieves enlightenment, even his chickens and dogs may ascend to heaven.

When one person succeeds, everyone around him prospers.

◈ **A similar English expression: Even a dog swaggers if its master wins favor.**

成语，贬义，表示一个人有了成就，周围的人也跟着有好处。通常用来指靠关系获利。

Idiom, derogatory, denoting that one person's success may beget favors and benefits for other related people; often used to criticize nepotism.

Examples:

我发现咱们公司新来的人里，好几个都是总经理的亲戚，这真是一人得道，鸡犬升天。

Of the new employees in our company, a couple of them are relatives of the general manager. Well, it is true that one man's achievement may bring fortune to those who are around him.

A：他大哥成为著名电视节目主持后，他在家乡也变得很有名气。
B：一人得道，鸡犬升天呀。
A: After his big brother became a famous TV show host, he also got quite popular in his hometown.
B: Surely, he gets a free ride from his brother's success.

Tips

1. 得道(dédào)：动宾短语，修行成功，领悟了道理；道，本指修行成功的境界；常用于表示取得了成就。
Verb-object phrase, to be enlightened, to gain enlightenment; (dào), enlightenment, the Way; often used to indicate to have attained high achievements.

yì shān róng bùdé èr hǔ
92. 一山 容不得 二虎

One mountain cannot accommodate two tigers.

◈ **There can be only one leader in a group.**

谚语，中性，强调双方竞争，只能有一方成功，另一方必然失败。通常用来说明双方会有激烈的竞争或者解释一方失败的原因。也可以说“一山不容二虎”。

Proverb, neutral, emphasizing that only one side can win, while the other loses; often used to indicate fierce competition will occur or to explain why one side lost. Also can say “一山不容二虎”.

Examples:

公司的两位副总一直是竞争对手。最近，其中一位副总离开了公司，毕竟一山容不得二虎。

The two vice presidents have always been rivals. Recently, one of them left. After all, one mountain cannot accommodate two tigers.

A：俗话说一山不容二虎。我和男朋友都属虎，将来在一起能和谐吗？

B：别迷信了。只要你们两人感情好，你不用担心。

A: The old saying goes that one mountain cannot accommodate two tigers. Both of my boyfriend and I are born in the year of tiger. Will we be able to have a harmonious family in the future?

B: Don't be superstitious. As long as you two love each other, you have nothing to worry.

Tips

1. 容(róng)：动词，古代汉语，包容，容忍。
   Verb, classical Chinese, to accommodate, to tolerate.
2. 和谐(héxié)：形容词，和睦，协调，没有对抗冲突。
   Adjective, harmonious, on good terms, coherent with.
3. 迷信(míxìn)：动词，盲目地相信。
   Verb, to believe blindly.

yì zhāo bèi shé yǎo shí nián pà jǐng shéng

93. 一朝 被蛇咬，十年怕井绳

Once bitten by a snake one will be afraid of a rope for ten years.

After a setback, people will lose confidence for a long time.

◈ **Similar English expressions: A burnt child dreads fire. Once bitten, twice shy.**

谚语，中性，表示受过伤害后就会对类似的事情特别敏感。通常用来解释一些人过分敏感的原因。

Proverb, neutral, denoting that anxieties that developed after a trauma or a setback might occur again in similar situations; often used to explain why people are obsessively cautious or sensitive to certain situations.

Examples:

我丈夫一生的积蓄都在股市里损失了。一朝被蛇咬，十年怕井绳，一提起股市，他就心情不安。

My husband lost all his savings in the stock market. He would become anxious every time when stock market is mentioned.

A：我十年前骑摩托，摔过一跤。现在早就不骑了。

B：你这是一朝被蛇咬，十年怕井绳啊。

A: I used to ride motorcycles ten years ago and had a serious accident, so I gave it up long ago.

B: I see your point. You are once bitten, twice shy.

Tips

1. 积蓄(jīxù):名词,积累下来的钱。
   Noun, savings.
2. 一A,就B(yī A, jiù B):表示两件事在时间上前后紧接着。
   Once A happens, then B will occur; denoting two things happen back to back.

yuǎn shuǐ jiě bù liǎo jìn kě

94. 远水解不了近渴

Distant water cannot quench immediate thirst.

Helps from afar cannot solve immediate problems.

◈ **A similar English expression: While the grass is growing, the horse is starving.**

谚语,中性,表示长远的计划解决不了目前的问题,或危机时刻得不到及时的帮助。通常用来强调必须及时想办法解决问题。

Proverb, neutral, denoting that a long-term plan cannot solve immediate problems, or an immediate help cannot be reached during a crisis; often used to emphasize the necessity of finding a more available and faster solution.

Examples:

外援一个月后才能到,远水解不了近渴,我们要自己想办法。

Foreign aid will not get here until one month later. Helps from afar cannot solve our immediate problem. We have to rely on ourselves now.

A：车偏偏坏在这个地方。咱们赶紧打救援电话吧？

B：打电话有什么用？这里远离大城市，远水解不了近渴。

A: We are really out of luck that the car is broke down right here. Let's call a roadside service.

B: There is no use. We're too far away from any major city and no repair people can reach us in time.

Tips

1. 偏偏(piānpiān)：副词，动作、行为或事情的发生，跟愿望、预料或常理相反。
Adverb, indicating that things happen against one's will or out of the normal.

2. 救援(jiùyuán)：动词，帮助、解救。
Verb, to aid, to rescue.

95. 有眼无珠 (yǒu yǎn wú zhū)

Having eyes but no eyeballs

◈ **Failed to recognize talented people or critical situations**

成语，贬义，表示完全没有辨别能力。通常用于严肃的批评。

Four-character idiom, derogatory,denoting that people are blind to the greatness of other people or objects; often used for severe criticism.

Examples:

他后悔自己有眼无珠，没有留住那个出色的球员。否则，他的球队就会赢得冠军了。

He regrets that his shortsightedness prevented him from keeping that outstanding player on his team. Otherwise, his team would have won the championship easily.

A：你们结婚前不是已经恋爱3年了吗？你怎么不知道他的问题？

B：别提了，都怪我有眼无珠，以前没看清他是什么样的人。

A: You had dated for 3 years before getting married, right? How come you didn' t know his problems?

B: I am truely shamed of it. It is my fault for not knowing him thoroughly before our marriage.

Tips

1. 球员(qiúyuán)：名词，从事球类运动的人。
   Noun, ball player.
2. 恋爱(liàn'ài)：动词，依恋，爱慕。
   Verb, to be in love, to date, to be serious with each other.
3. 怪(guài)：动词，批评，责备。
   Verb, to criticize, to blame.

Z

zǎixiàng dùlǐ néng chēng chuán

96. 宰相 肚里能 撑 船

A boat can sail in the belly of a prime minister.

◈ **Great people are tolerant and forgiving.**

谚语，褒义，强调需要有足够的容忍度。通常用于称赞他人的容忍度很高。

Proverb, commendatory, emphasizing people's leniency; often used to praise people for their high tolerance to others.

Examples:

在处理人际关系时，我们要抱着宰相肚里能撑船的态度，宽容别人的缺点。

When it comes to social interactions, we must always keep an open mind towards others and be tolerant.

A: 老张真是宰相肚里能撑船，他决定与当初的对手合作。

B: 但只要仔细分析一下就知道，这是政治的需要。

A: Mr. Zhang is indeed a very broad minded person. He has decided to collaborate with his rival.

B: But if you look closely, you'll see that it's simply a political maneuver.

Tips

1. 人际关系(rénjì guānxi):名词,人和人之间的关系。人际,人和人之间的;关系,相互作用、相互影响。

   Noun, interpersonal relations; rénjì, interpersonal; guānxi, relations.

2. 撑(chēng):动词,用竹竿使船前进。

   Verb, to pole (a boat).

3. 宽容(kuānróng):动词,容易原谅理解别人;形容词,不计较。

   Verb, to tolerate; adjective, tolerable.

4. 宰相(zǎixiàng):名词,中国古代政府总理的称号。

   Noun, the title for prime minister in ancient China.

5. 分析(fēnxī):动词,研究找出事物之间的内在联系。

   Verb, to analyze, to find out inner connections or causal relations among things.

zhēng yī zhī yǎn bì yī zhī yǎn

97. 睁一只眼闭一只眼

To keep one eye open and the other closed

◈ **To turn a blind eye toward something**

谚语,中性,表示不要过分严格执行规定,对某些事应该容忍。

Proverb, neutral, denoting not being very serious or vigilant in implementing controls, or being tolerant to something.

Examples:

食品安全事关重大。作为检察官，我绝不能睁一只眼闭一只眼。

Food safety is very important. As an inspector, I cannot turn a blind eye to possible safety violations.

A：街头小贩是弱势群体，让他们在街边卖点东西好了。

B：税务局也许会睁一只眼闭一只眼，可是他们不能影响交通啊。

A: Street peddlers are an underprivileged group; maybe it is not bad to allow them to sell something freely by street corners.

B: The tax authorities may turn a blind eye towards them, but they should not cause any traffic problems.

Tips

1. 事关重大(shìguānzhòngdà)：四字短语，(事情)会产生重要的影响。

   Four-character phrase, things are crucial and important.

2. 检察官(jiǎncháguān)：名词，负责进行调查取证用来提起诉讼的人。

   Noun, public prosecutor.

3. 小贩(xiǎofàn)：名词，在路边做小生意的人。

   Noun, peddler; small vender.

4. 弱势群体(ruòshì qúntǐ)：名词，社会中影响力小收入低的人群。
Noun, underprivileged group, people with low-income and little influence.

zhīma kāi huā jié jié gāo
98. 芝麻 开花——节节高

Sesames are blooming—going up notch by notch.

◈ **Things are developing very well.**

歇后语，褒义，表示越来越好。通常用来称赞或者祝愿好的事情越来越多。

Two-part allegorical saying, commendatory, denoting things are getting better; often used in a congratulatory speech.

Examples:

中国改革开放三十年，人民的生活是芝麻开花——节节高呀。

After China's reforms thirty years ago, people's lives have been getting better and better.

A：星期日我的饭店开张大吉，请你一定要来喝一杯酒啊。

B：好。我先祝你的生意芝麻开花，节节高啊！

A: My restaurant is opening this Sunday. Please come for a drink.

B: Sure. I wish your business one success after another.

Tips

1. 节(jié)：量词，竹子、甘蔗、芝麻等植物的茎的一部分。
   Measure word, a section, a notch, as often seen in bamboo, sugar cane, and sesame plant.
2. 开张大吉(kāizhāng dà jí)：成语，用来祝贺商店、饭馆等一开始就有一个好的经营。
   Four-character idiom, best luck to the grand opening; often used to express good wills to a new business.

zhǐ lǐ bāo bú zhù huǒ

99. 纸里包不住火

Fire cannot be contained in paper.

◈ The truth cannot be concealed.

谚语，中性，形容坏的事情一定会暴露。通常强调坏人一定会被抓住，隐藏的事物一定会被发现。

Proverb, neutral, indicating that bad things will be disclosed for sure; often used to emphasizing a bad situation will not last long.

Examples:

纸里包不住火。他抄袭别人文章的事最终被发现了。

Like fire cannot be contained in paper, the fact that he plagiarized is eventually disclosed.

A：我没有告诉家里人被解聘的事。
B：纸里包不住火，他们早晚都会知道的。
A: I have not told my family that I was laid off.
B: You can't keep this secret forever. They will eventually find it out.

Tips

1. 抄袭(chāoxí)：动词，把别人的成果完全拿过来自己用。
   Verb, to plagiarize.
2. 最终(zuìzhōng)：副词，事情的最后阶段。
   Adverb, finally, at last.
3. 解聘(jiěpìn)：动词，解除聘用关系；解，解除；聘，聘用（关系）。
   Verb, to terminate one's employment, to lay off; jiě, to remove, to release; pìn, as in pìnyòng, employment.
4. 早晚(zǎowǎn)：副词，（事情）或早或晚，但是一定会发生。
   Adverb, sooner or later, eventually.

100. 竹篮打水——一场空
zhú lán dǎ shuǐ　yì chǎng kōng

Getting water with a bamboo basket— with empty results

◈ **Efforts made in vain**

歇后语，贬义，强调付出最终没有任何的回报。通常用于对无效付出的彻底否定。

Two-part allegorical saying, derogatory, emphasizing a lack of reward or return after efforts; often used to indicate efforts in vain.

Examples:

他一大早就爬到山顶去看日出，结果是竹篮打水——一场空。因为雾太大，什么也没看到。

He climbed up to the mountain top in the early morning in order to see the sunrise. But the efforts turned out in vain. Because of heavy fog, he couldn't see anything at all.

A：我学习了很久，想通过那个考试。可是没有通过。真是竹篮打水一场空啊。

B：别着急，再努力一下，你会通过的。

A: I studied for a long in order to pass the exam. But I failed, with all efforts made in vain.

B: No worry. If you keep studying hard, you will pass it.

Tips

1. 一大早(yídàzǎo)：口语，早上很早的时候。
   Colloquial, early in the morning.
2. 日出(rìchū)：名词，太阳升起。
   Noun, sunrise.
3. 雾(wù)：名词，空气中的水气。
   Noun, fog, mist.
4. 竹篮(zhúlán)：名词，竹子做的篮子。竹，竹子；篮，篮子。
   Noun, bamboo basket; zhú, bamboo; lán, short for lánzi, basket.